Suicide and the Eternal Nature of the Soul

Suicide and the Eternal Nature of the Soul

Anonymous

Worldwide United Publishing
Melba, Idaho

Suicide and the Eternal Nature of the Soul

December 2, 2023
First Edition

SOFTCOVER ISBN: 978-1-937390-42-6

Library of Congress Control Number: 2023945145

Worldwide United Publishing
an imprint of Pearl Publishing, LLC
2587 Southside Blvd., Melba, ID 83641
www.pearlpublishing.net—1.888.499.9666

CONTENTS

INTRODUCTION

So ... you've thought about ending your life.

You have your reasons. No one really understands these reasons except YOU. There might be a few people (some who even seem to be sincere) who *claim* to understand why you're thinking this way. But do they really? Do they really understand why you want to take your life?

No, they DO NOT understand! IF they did, they would be able to help *you* change your mind to keep on living.

This planet truly is a lone and dreary world. No matter how hard you've tried to accept your life on Earth, your existence here just doesn't seem to be bringing you the happiness that you have yearned for. Besides this intense longing for happiness, you may have also wondered, "Who am I?" and "Why do I exist?"

You may have heard many different answers to these questions. But probably none of them have made much sense to you. Furthermore, none of these so-called answers have helped you feel comfortable with YOU, or given you a sense that your life really *is* worth living.

If you've thought about (or are thinking about) ending your life, this book is for you. Before you end your existence on this earth, give this book a chance.

The purpose of this book is not to change your mind immediately. One book shouldn't have that type of power over you. Your thoughts about ending your life (and your possible *decision* to do so) prove just how much power YOU have over YOUR own existence. No one has the power to stop you from taking your own life.

As mentioned above, you might know some sincere family members, friends, teachers, preachers, or counselors who claim they want to help you. But have any of these people given you the answers to the questions that you can't help but ponder? Again, "Who am I? Why do I exist?"

Obviously, you have not yet heard or found any answers that are satisfying—or any that have *convinced you* that your life *is* worth living. If those sincere people in your life had provided such an answer, you wouldn't still be thinking about ending your life.

Ending your life is pretty easy to do, though. Many have done it before you. Many will do it while you are reading this book. Even more will do it in the next second, in the next minute, in the next hour, in the next day, in the next week, and in the next year. The suicide rate is rising throughout this world and no one seems to know what to do about it.

Our hope is that after considering the information provided in this book, you will find the power within your Self to change your *own* mind. This should be done by your*self,* without being manipulated in any way, by anyone.

You know what other people have said. You've heard their encouragement to "keep on keeping on." But nothing *they* have said has helped you. You still feel hopeless, living in a lonely and unexciting world. Perhaps what they have said *is* the problem.

You have heard from *them*! But have you heard the Real Truth® about who you are and why you exist?

There are all kinds of *truths*. Everyone thinks their opinion of *truth* is right. And it shouldn't be too surprising to realize that, in the process of thinking they're right, they must also think that everyone else is wrong. Could it be possible that *everyone* is right, which makes everyone wrong?

Consider all the *truths* that other people embrace, many times trying to convince you that *only theirs* is acceptable. The constant arguments and heated discussions you've heard are a mass of confusion. Do any of *their truths* answer your questions about who you are and why you exist?

It is entirely reasonable to feel sick and tired of people not being able to answer your questions. They present *their truths*; but when you have questions about *their truths*, they cannot offer satisfactory answers. This discourages you and adds to the mass of confusion already inside of your head. This may have resulted in feelings of wanting to end this confusion (and sometimes the thought of committing suicide seems like the only sure way).

We propose that there actually *is* a *real truth*. Thus, with total confidence, the publisher has registered this idea of *real truth* as a trademark, distinguishing it from all other supposed *truths* on Earth.

The Real Truth® is defined as things as they *really* are in the present, as they *really* were in the past, and as they *really* will be in the future. If something is Real Truth®, then it is the same today as it was thousands of years ago, and as it will continue to be true tomorrow and forever.

We claim to have the Real Truth® about who you are and why you exist. We claim that it can answer ALL of your questions, leaving none unanswered. It can make sense out of all the confusion caused by *their truths*—*their ideas* and *beliefs* that have turned the human *earth experience* into a lone and dreary world. We promise to give you some examples of things as they *really* are concerning your existence as a human being. We promise to answer *all* of your questions about these things.

Before you burden yourself with reading this entire book, consider the following example of this Real Truth® that we hope will inspire you to keep reading:

Science currently claims that the sun will eventually burn out and all life and existence on the earth will end. It also has its *theories* about gravity and magnetism, which are just two of many examples. However, scientific *theories* (*their truths*) do not *really* present conclusive answers that remain the same throughout time. Keep in mind, there was a time in the not-too-distant past when science believed the earth was flat and that the sun revolved around it.

When someone finally and courageously stood up and presented a *different* idea about the sun and the earth, this brave soul was not well liked. This fearless one (and others like him) stood against the prevailing *truth* of the past. This unorthodox idea (that the earth revolves around the sun and not the other way around) not only made a lot more sense, but also has not changed for the hundreds of years that have followed. It was the same in the past as it is today— and it will be forever and ever: the earth revolves around the sun. This is the Real Truth®.

As previous scientific theories have been proven wrong, so, too, can the current scientific theory about the sun. The Real Truth® is that the sun is *not* burning out. Imagine that we had the ability to travel back in time billions of years with a machine that could measure the exact amount of energy (light and heat) that the sun gives off. If we could do this, we would find that the amount of heat and light produced by the sun has *not* changed for billions of years and is still the same today.

The sun was created in and of space matter (science likes to call it *dark matter*). To maintain itself, the sun continually pulls in dark matter. This is similar to a nuclear reactor, which requires fuel rods to sustain its power and efficiency. These rods need to be changed from time to time to keep the reactor the same yesterday as it is today, and as it will be in the future. In like manner, the sun's "fuel rods" are the dark matter from which it was created.

As the sun draws in dark matter to maintain itself, whatever else is found in the dark matter is also sucked in. This natural occurrence creates a force known as a *gravitational pull*. So, the next obvious question is: "Why aren't all the planets (including Earth) being sucked into the sun and consumed, along with the dark matter that fuels the sun's existence?" So as not to disappoint you so early on in your reading, here is that answer:

Each planet has a nuclear-like reactor in the center of it (i.e., its core). Each planet was made of the same space material (*dark matter*) as the sun. The difference between the planets and the sun is that the sun doesn't need the planets in order to exist. The planets, however, *do* need the sun. The energy created by the sun makes the planets do what they do while orbiting around the sun.

The sun's energy comes from a fusion process, taking dark matter to create ordinary matter. The energy from this process is also used in the creation of the planets. Each planet was created to act and be acted upon by the sun's energy. Each planet's nuclear core generates movement of energy (like a magnet). This creates a magnetic field.

Two magnets maintain an equilibrium between each other by repelling or attracting (pushing or pulling). In the case of celestial objects (planets and stars), the magnetic field between a sun and a planet causes them to repel each other. This keeps the planet from being sucked toward the sun beyond a scientifically pre-determined distance.

Each planet is created according to a precise mathematical algorithm (process) that determines how strong its magnetic field will be. In our solar system, Jupiter's magnetic field was created to be much stronger than Earth's. Thus, Jupiter's distance from the sun is further than Earth's.

This revelation about *gravity* and *magnetism* is the Real Truth®. But it is *not* accepted, yet, by science. Why? Because it proves that the entire scientific community and *its truths* are wrong. It is PRIDE that keeps science from automatically accepting explanations that make sense—that answer all of the questions about gravity and magnetism.

When science finally figures out how to create a new planet from *dark matter*, it will have figured out the mathematical algorithm (process) that will keep this new planet at a precise distance from the sun. This will be done according to the purpose for which the new planet is created. The two examples given above—*things as they really are*—prove that science isn't always correct.

Religion is not correct either. At this point in the introduction, dealing with *all* the *beliefs* associated with religion would not be reasonable. (Like science, *their truths* are also ever changing, but even more confusing.) However, because religious beliefs are the main cause of many suicides, these issues *must* be considered as very important and will be properly addressed in this book.

This book *will* answer questions about who you are and why you exist. It will provide you with the Real Truth®. These answers have never been given before. These answers will stand the test of time. These answers were the same in the past as they are today, and as they will be forever ... worlds without end.

It's pretty easy to write a few paragraphs that make such bold claims. However, the only way you'll be convinced that the answers provided make sense and end your confusion IS TO FINISH READING THIS BOOK. We invite you to keep reading.

(PLEASE NOTE: A very important thing to consider is that the answers given in this book are provided for FREE to everyone. This book can easily be downloaded without cost. Furthermore, the authors do not want to be known or to receive any accolade or praise. These two facts should be somewhat refreshing from what you've experienced so far.)

The answers given in this book still might not change your mind about ending your existence on Earth. Perhaps knowing the Real Truth® about who you are and why you exist will actually cause you to be even more sure about ending your own life. But, at least in understanding things as they *really* are, you can make a more informed decision ... again, a decision that *only you* can make for yourself.

However, if this book serves its purpose, you will be convinced that *YOU ARE* worth saving, and that your life upon this earth IS worth living. That said, remember that there is no one on Earth who has the right to decide whether or not you stay alive, except YOU!

The information provided in this book has some incredible redeeming power. It has the power to save you! Obviously, if you're thinking about ending your existence, you haven't received the right kind of information—information that might help you answer the question: "To live or not to live?"

Whatever information you have already received—whatever you have learned throughout your life on Earth—has led you to contemplate the possibility that it would be better for you *not* to exist. Again, you have the power to make this choice; and no one has the power to make any decision for you, except YOU.

The people in your life who do not want you to end your existence ... to end your associations with them ... are likely *not* going to appreciate the information given in this book—ironically, not even if the information saves your life.

PRIDE holds the human mind in chains of captivity. The philosophies of the world, mingled with the published writings of both science and religion, can create a mass of confusion in your mind. And science and religion are not going to surrender easily. Upon reading this book, you might decide to keep on living because of the information it provides. Nonetheless, because these Real Truths® counter *their truths*, you might very well be rejected and mocked for considering and accepting it. Facing the PRIDE of this world might convince you (yes, even more so) that life is *not* worth living among such ignorant people.

The *prideful* people who have lost a loved one to suicide will likely *not* accept the information given in this book. Why? Because it will discount *their truths*. It will provide information that proves, beyond any reasonable doubt, what the human soul *really* is, and that it is *eternal*—always has been and always will be— worlds without end.

———————————

As you read further, you will learn that YOU continue to exist *after* your mortal body has returned to the dust from which it was created on planet Earth. You will learn that whoever YOU are *after* you die, is the exact same person YOU were ... the REAL YOU ... *before* you were born into a mortal body on this earth. You will also come to understand that the *you* who was created through the sexual process of two other people passing on their DNA, has absolutely nothing to do with the eternal nature of your individual soul.

This can be quite disturbing to people who have lost a loved one. These hopeful ones want to see their loved one again, in the same physical body in which their cherished one existed on Earth (and with which they experienced their mortal relationship). Nevertheless, the Real Truth® does not conform to the imaginations that the mortal human mind makes up. If the *real you* exists *after* your mortal body is gone, then common sense dictates that this *real you* existed *before* the mortal body was created by two earth-based parents. In other words, if there is such a thing as a pre-mortal life, then your post-mortal life must be the same—which it is. This is the Real Truth®.

Let's cater to religion for a moment. There is a particular church with an abnormally high rate of suicide among its members. Per capita, they take more antidepressants than any other group of people currently living on Earth. Leaders of this religion struggle to answer simple questions about who we are and why we exist. Because of this ignorance, this religion contributes to the mass of confusion that already causes a person to question the value of their life.

Below is a quote of scripture from this church's website. The quote, as written, makes a lot of sense about *life* and mortal *death*. Unfortunately, the quote contradicts the *teachings* of the religion mentioned above, who *claim* to accept it as *their truth*, as *their* scripture, as *their* "Word of God":

> Now, concerning the state of the soul between death and the resurrection—Behold, it has been made known unto me by an angel, that

the spirits of all men, as soon as they are departed from this mortal body, yea, the spirits of all men, whether they be good or evil, are taken home to that God who gave them life.

The same religious group that maintains the above passage as *their truth* (despite their differing teachings), also claims that the mortal man *Adam* was once a god called *Michael*. Carefully considered, this assertion contradicts *their truth* that states:

"As man is, God once was; as God is, man may become."

Michael is the one who had life and consciousness *before* being put into a deep sleep, where he started dreaming that he was the man *Adam* living in a "lone and dreary world." Therefore, *their truth* should say:

"As God is, man once was; and as God is, man may become again."

This idea that, "As God (*Michael*) is, man (*Adam*) once was; and as God is, man may become again," was originally taught purposefully in this religion's sacred ordinances. But it contradicts this religion's more modern doctrine that "Families Are Forever." If, upon death, a mortal person is "taken home to that God who gave them life," then the Earth-parents, who gave them *mortal* life, are nonconsequential to that person's eternal existence. (We will continue to deal with both scientific and religious *truths* in upcoming chapters.)

In order for you to feel that life *is* worth living, and that existing as a conscious human being on Earth has a personal purpose for you, the Real Truth® about who you are and why you exist must be answered. It must make sense. No other questions can remain.

So, what is the Real Truth® about the human soul? The "soul" described herein is the power of *consciousness*. The information offered in this book will prove that, unless a physical body is conscious of its environment, there is no "soul" connected to it. The physical body *is*, however, still able to function by itself in the environment in which it was created and exists. (For example, while the body is only a fetus in a womb, it can have reflexes and a heartbeat but does not have a "soul" connected to it.)

Consciousness means that a physical body can *receive energy from* the environment in which it exists, AND *give off energy* (emit it) back into the same environment. A physical body alone cannot do this (for instance, a baby in a womb, or a body after a person dies). *Consciousness* allows an entity (a physical body made of the same elements that exist in the environment) to act upon this environment (world) and to be acted upon by the same.

The soul is *not* consciousness. It is the *energy* that allows you to exist on any particular planet in a physical body. This energy allows the body to maintain a constant interaction with the surrounding world. Better said, *the soul is the power of consciousness.* The physical body is *not* the soul. The physical body allows the soul, not only to exist, but also to operate and perform (i.e., to see, hear, taste, touch, smell, think, and breathe) in the world in which it *does* exist.

An infant body developing in the womb is *not* conscious. If a developing body had the *power* to become conscious, it would be a very sad day for the infant if it *woke up* inside the womb. Furthermore, the infant body does not and cannot act *toward* or react *with* the environment while developing inside the mother's womb in the same way that the body of the mother acts toward and reacts with her environment. Hence, the mother is conscious, and the infant (while in the womb) is not.

The particular Christian religion we mentioned above* believes that Jesus Christ appeared a *second time* in his resurrected glory. It teaches that Jesus Christ was born among the Jews in the Eastern Hemisphere. Then, after his death and resurrection, he also appeared in the Western Hemisphere to the people living there. A scripture specifically written to address this concept describes a prophet living in the Western Hemisphere prophesying about the birth of Jesus in the Eastern Hemisphere.

According to the story, the day before Jesus' *soul* was put into the body created for him in Bethlehem (located in the Eastern Hemisphere), his *eternal soul* was speaking to an ancient American prophet:

> Lift up your head and be of good cheer; for behold, the time is at hand, and on this night shall the sign be given, and on the morrow come I into the world.

This narrative about the mortal life of Jesus clearly demonstrates that his *true self* was *not* in the world while his mortal body was in his mother's womb: "on the morrow come I into the world." Where was Jesus *before* he came into the world?

(*NOTE: Again, we have chosen the above-mentioned religion, without specifically naming it, because of how many of its members use antidepressants and commit suicide. It is obvious that the contradicting doctrines taught by this particular religion add to an emotional distress that contributes to suicide.)

This scripture referenced above *should* convince these religious believers that the *eternal soul* does *not* enter the body until the day of birth. In contrast, most religious people believe that the *soul* enters the body upon conception.

(Abortion rights are a popular topic of discussion and contention that divides humanity and causes undue stress on many lives. Many young girls who have had an abortion have been convinced that they murdered another human being. A few of these girls later committed suicide because of the guilt they felt. It is our hope to mitigate [lessen] this guilt.)

The infant's body does not exist in the womb *until* it begins to develop (commencing when an egg and a sperm join, then becoming the embryo, and later, the fetus). The *environment* from which the fetal body is created is provided by the mother's womb. Unlike the *unconscious* fetus, the parent is conscious. This is determined by the ability of the parent's body being able to take in energy and release energy back into the environment in which the parent exists. The parent is a *living soul*. The fetus is *not*.

Soon, advancements in technology and science will allow for the creation of a physical body *outside* of a female's womb. Such an *artificial womb* must have the ability to interact with the environment in order to suck in energy and pass it on to the developing body. This will allow the physical body to form and grow.

Some might suppose that this *artificial womb* will meet the criteria of a *soul*... because it has the power to act upon the environment in which it exists. This is *not* Real Truth®. Therefore, it is very important to understand another crucial part of defining a *soul*.

A *soul* has the power to act on its own. A *living soul* is not dependent on any outside influence or power acting upon it to control it or tell it what it can and cannot do in any given environment. In other words, the *soul* is *living* because it has *free will*.

An *artificial womb* does not and cannot have free will. The inventors, engineers, and technicians that will develop the *artificial womb* will create and program it to do *their* will. Additionally, a fetus developing inside an *artificial womb* does not and cannot have free will.

However, when the developed physical body is released from its *artificial environment* (the artificial womb), the person(s) who is/are responsible for the artificial womb will no longer have any control over this body. This release from being bound to the womb is indicated by the new body taking its first breath. At this point, it begins to act and be acted upon *solely* by itself and of its own existence, with free will.

15

Again, the two requirements for the existence of the *soul* are:

1) To have the power to act upon and be acted upon by the environment in which it exists; and,

2) To make the free-willed choice to act in and react to the environment.

Therefore, when a *physical body* has the power to consciously make free-willed decisions to act and allow itself to be acted upon by the environment in which it exists—without any other thing acting upon it—the body then is a *living soul.* Outside of either the parent's womb or the *artificial* womb, the physical body no longer needs the womb, or the person (or thing) that provided the womb.

For example, upon adoption by another person, infants are taken away from the person who provided the womb. Anyone can feed and care for the newly created body. But the infant still has the free-willed choice to eat or not. This is different from the time the body was developing in the womb, when the body had *no free will* and could not make any choices of its own. Above was written:

[Those] who have lost a loved one to suicide will likely *not* accept the information given in this book. Why? Because it will discount *their truths.* It will provide information that proves, beyond any reasonable doubt, what the human soul *really* is, and that it is *eternal.*

The information in this book will likewise offend people who believe that the only proper way for a human body to be created is in the womb of a parent. To these people, the accepted gender of a person who has a womb in which a human body can form, is generally recognized as *female* (in contrast to a *male*, who does not have a womb). These believe a god designed a childbearing person's body for that very purpose—to bear children. The idea of a god suggests that a *power* exists outside of and above a mortal human's free will.

The advent of the *artificial womb* will soon negate the need for a female's womb. Furthermore, as new human bodies are engineered to resist sickness and aging, the *artificial* womb will replace and be accepted as a better option than mortal womb-created bodies.

Science can explain how *chromosomes* work, starting with molecules of amino acids that create proteins, which create DNA, which produces bodies—not only of humans, but of all living things. As you understand further how life is created, allowing for the creation of new life in an artificial womb, the idea of a supernatural god will not make much sense any longer. For this reason, religion fights science and its advancements and innovations that take the place of a god.

———————

Despite the advancements in science, most people who commit suicide hold religious beliefs as their standards and values, when they consider and contemplate the worth of their existence. Therefore, we will utilize a lot of religious ideologies.

If you're contemplating suicide because of some confusion associated with your personal religious beliefs, continue reading. You will discover ideas that will truly set you free from the bondage and chains of hell created by the religions found on this earth. For example, consider the following:

Many people believe there exists a power outside of the human *soul*—a supernatural power that has more supremacy over a person than the person has over their own Self. Those who believe this should consider that this outside force or power (God) has done *nothing*, and can do *nothing*, to keep a person from committing suicide. These people should also consider and examine their own beliefs, especially those who believe in Judeo-Christian-Islamic scripture.

One might ask: "How did *their* God create the first human named Adam? Was sex involved? In whose womb did Adam's body develop?" According to the story, Eve (the first woman) did not exist before Adam (the first man). The Bible's narrative explains clearly that Eve's body came from Adam's body. Therefore, as the story goes, the first male's body created the first female's body.

How did God do this? How did God create the first physical bodies for the *earth experience*? Could it have been that the first body ... Adam's ... was non-binary (ungendered)? What was the actual process that occurred that allowed God to create the first human bodies? These questions will be answered as you begin to learn Real Truth®.

Moreover (and most importantly), according to the Bible's story, a woman was "cursed" to experience pain in child bearing. The way that women have children currently—in this *cursed* (fallen) world ... is certainly very painful. But this way was a "curse," and not how God created Adam and Eve in *His own way*, with God's intelligence ... according to these religious beliefs.

If God were to ever take away this "curse," how then would new human bodies be created from the "dust of the earth"? Although people miss it, if understood correctly, the Bible does in fact explain that, in the beginning, God did *not* intend for people to experience pain in childbearing, nor for a female to be subservient to and dominated by a male.

The above-mentioned people cannot answer these simple and logical observations and critical examinations of their beliefs. They will be offended by analyzing their own Bible's story. Additionally, those who have lost a loved one to suicide will be even more offended, as it is proven beyond any doubt that the *human soul* is an ETERNAL ENTITY OF POWER (ENERGY).

It will be proven that the *power of the soul* has nothing to do with the body created from the DNA patterns passed on by mortal parents, who, according to the aforementioned religious beliefs, are *cursed*. This power of consciousness is *eternal, without beginning and without end*. Therefore, it was exactly the same *before* connecting to a mortal, Earth-bound body, as it will continue to be *after* disconnecting from this body through death.

Most people who report having a *near-death* experience sense that they have left their mortal body. Some relate that they have seen their mortal body lying dead. Who are they when they are seeing their physical body lying dead? What are they? Why are they floating? How are they floating and moving throughout some sort of environment (space) outside of their Earth-bound body? Whoever or whatever these conscious entities are, gravity and any of the other laws associated with the earth seem to have no effect on their continued conscious, presumably physical *post-mortal Self.*

If you have experienced the death of a young loved one, you may find comfort in believing that one day you will see this person again, and that they will look just like they did before they died. Let's examine the logic of this. As an example, let's suppose that you're a young couple and your partner dies in their early 30s. Your hope is that you will see that person again someday in the *hereafter.* Let's assume you continue to live until you're in your 80s, having other loving relationships with other partners. When you die, are you going to see your former partner still in their 30s, while you're now in your 80s?

Your grandchildren see you alive in your 80s; and that's the only memory they have of you before you die. If being their grandparent was the only relationship that meant anything to them, when they meet you after death, are you going to be *their* 80-year-old grandparent? Or are you going to appear 30 again, continuing your relationship with your partner who died in their early 30s, discounting the other relationships that you had after your partner died?

This book will prove that the *conscious YOU*, which will continue to exist after the mortal You dies, is the exact same *being* ... the exact same *soul* ... the *exact same power* ... that YOU always were, that you are, and that you always will be.

This information will greatly offend those who receive comfort and hope from the belief that one day they will see their loved ones again. This information will also prove that the *You* who you are while living consciously upon the earth, making your own decisions according to what you are experiencing on Earth, will NEVER exist again after you die.

This is a very hard concept for a lot of people to accept. Those who benefit or profit from the idea that you will continue to look like and be the same person you are while living upon Earth, will fight this information. But again, *their* information, *their* beliefs, and *their* opinions about human existence have not helped you decide *not* to end your existence. Furthermore, it adds to the mass of confusion that has led you to contemplate this.

If the information given in this book does not change your mind, then perhaps you're making the right choice to end your life ... a life you feel is without hope or purpose. Your suicide will end the life of a person who, taking all things into consideration, hopelessly lives upon Earth. However, our commitment to you, because you're taking the time to read this information, is that it will give you the proper knowledge so that you can make the right decision of whether to be or not to be, a decision that only you can make.

Again, not to seem counterproductive to our hope, perhaps it *would be* better for you to end your existence upon this earth. Perhaps ending your current relationships with those who have not helped you decide to continue living, would be a better choice. HOWEVER, by the end of this book, it is hoped that you will begin to see your relationships with others differently, and also gain a brand-new perspective on your relationship with the *earth experience*.

Don't kill yourself until you have given this whole book a chance. Regardless of the information herein, no one can make that decision but you. Again, *YOU* have the power to end your life, or to save it. *YOU* have a power over YOU that no one else living on Earth, nor existing anywhere else in the universe, has over you or can take away from you. *YOU* are the Creator of your own destiny. *YOU*, and YOU alone, will determine whether or not your conscious existence upon planet Earth will end or continue.

No one else knows what you're going through. Yeah, many will tell you that they understand and want to help you. But you have probably already realized that they don't understand you. Because if they did, they would have been able to convince you *not* to end YOU.

You already know what others say about suicide. You've heard opinions from your parents, your teachers, your friends, and even from lots of strangers. How do these people, especially the strangers, know what you're going through?

Sure, therapists, psychologists, doctors, religious and spiritual leaders have done their best to convince you that your life is worth living. But what they've really tried to convince you of is that *your life* is worth something *to them*. Your loved ones don't want to feel the pain or guilt of losing you. If they do lose you, they might partially blame themselves for contributing to your decision to end your life.

The strangers have been *paid* to give you advice and counsel, not only in money, but also in the honor and respect they receive from others because of their titles. The *strangers* in this world give all kinds of advice; and there are all kinds of people making money off your desire to take your own life.

If you don't feel valued by others, or you feel you no longer have a purpose in life, tell everyone that you are going to commit suicide. Watch how fast your parents react to get you help. Watch how fast a therapist, psychologist, spiritual or religious leader suddenly takes interest in you. They will smile, speak softly, and do everything they can to convince you that they care about you. They might even put you in an institution, take away your free will, and force you to live.

You'll get lots of attention from people who sincerely want to help you. But you know better. You know that you would not be receiving any of their help or attention if you hadn't threatened to end your life. Where were these people with their outpouring of love and understanding while you were going through the troubles that made you consider ending your existence in the first place?

You're certainly not alone in your desire to end your life. Suicide rates have increased dramatically over the years. These rates are continuing to increase, despite how many books and articles have been written containing information that the authors hope and believe will help. The increasing number of mental health "experts" hasn't lowered the number of suicides. No matter how much study and effort has gone into trying to help people decide not to end their life, it appears instead that this effort could be part of the problem.

It shouldn't surprise you to find out that most therapists go to their own therapist, because of their inability to deal with their *own* mental issues. Aren't these people supposed to be giving YOU advice to help YOU with *your* problems? If these so-called experts are seeing other "experts" to help them, how can you trust that what your therapist is telling you will work for YOU? If their wisdom and advice is going to work for you, then obviously it should work for them. The science of mental health has failed you if you have listened to these strangers but still want to end your life.

But what about religion? Have spiritual guides, gurus, prophets, seers, and revelators made a difference in your decision? If these truly made a difference, the suicide rates among religious believers (devotees to religion) wouldn't be going up. And again, it shouldn't surprise you to find out that the majority of people who end their life ARE RELIGIOUS.

Religious people try asking for God's help. When their perceived God doesn't answer them or intervene in some supernatural (God-like) way, they feel that not even God cares if they end their life or not.

Most religious leaders do not want to lose you though. They have invented all kinds of concepts to convince you to continue living. Some have even threatened you with eternal damnation, attempting to stop you.

On the other hand, some religious leaders in the world have actually *promoted* suicide as a way to please God and help God do His work. Using common sense, you might question, "If sacrificing MY life to please God and fulfill His commandments is good, then why wouldn't these religious leaders sacrifice their *own* lives for the greater good? Why do I have to die for God, and my religious leaders do not?"

You might be aware of the Christian belief that God came down to Earth in the form of a mortal man and sacrificed his life for you. (Some call this the Atonement.) The belief that God gave His life for you should convince you that you don't need to sacrifice your own life to gain eternal salvation; God has already saved you.

Unfortunately, despite this very popular belief, this Christian god seems to be giving people commandments that lead them to suicide. Suicidal Christians are unable to find happiness in following Christian commandments—not mandates given in the Jesus story, but commandments from men who claim to have a connection with Jesus that you don't have. In reality, your fear of God is based entirely upon the precepts (ideas and teachings) of these men.

If you've read the Jesus story, you might have thought it would be a good thing if there actually was a god like Jesus. You would hope this god would teach the same things Jesus himself taught others, as the story describes. Sadly, this is not what Christians teach and believe. It would be wonderful to hope that the same Jesus of whom the stories are told would come again to the earth and wipe out all of your fears and anxiety.

The problem with ALL Christian religions is that they honor the man (Jesus) with their lips, but their hearts are far from him. Again, the fear that people have toward Jesus is taught and instilled in them by the ideas and teachings of men.

Consider the following Judeo-Christian-Islamic scripture:

> For the Lord hath poured out upon you the spirit of deep sleep, and hath closed your eyes: the prophets and your rulers, the seers hath he covered.

> Wherefore the Lord said, Forasmuch as this people draw near *me* with their mouth, and with their lips do honour me, but have removed their heart far from me, and their fear toward me is taught by the precept of men:

> Therefore, behold, I will proceed to do a marvelous work among this people, *even* a marvelous work and a wonder: for the wisdom of their wise *men* shall perish, and the understanding of their prudent *men* shall be hid.

Woe unto them that seek deep to hide their counsel from the LORD, and their works are in the dark, and they say, Who seeth us? And who knoweth us?

Surely your turning of things upside down shall be esteemed as the potter's clay: for shall the work say of him that made it, He made me not? Or shall the thing framed say of him that framed it, He had no understanding?

Consider the above scripture in relation to the ignorance of religious leaders (who are in a "deep sleep"). Surely, their hidden and private acts will one day be known.

Wouldn't it be advantageous to you ... while considering if your life is worth living ... if someone would introduce a "*marvelous work and a wonder*"? What if this information countered all the *"wise and prudent men"* who have been giving you counsel, but who have not been able to persuade you to continue to live? We hope this book becomes part of this marvelous work and a wonder for YOU. (It already is part of a Marvelous Work and a Wonder®.)

The best efforts of historians and news reporters prove that religion has created more war and death than any other human belief system. Believing that there is life after death will not help you decide whether or not to take your life. In fact, if you believe there *is* life after death, then you're more likely to rely on this faith and commit suicide (hoping that the next life is better than this one).

If you finish this book and read it with an open mind, a sincere heart, and with real intent to see if the information offered will help you make the right decision, you will find that the information surpasses and transcends science and religion. The information is much more logical than anything that science and religion have to offer.

So, if science and religion can't help you answer the question you are pondering—"To be or not to be"—what can? Who can help you? Again, there's only one person who can save you. Only YOU can save you!

Using common sense might help you make a rational decision about your existence. However, you must first *consider* new information that makes more sense than anything you've ever considered before.

———————

Because you are human, you have the ability to reason and think differently from all other life forms that exist. Keep in mind that there is no other life form (besides a human) that contemplates suicide and is faced with making an informed decision about ending its life. It's our human ability to make this "informed decision" that separates us from all other life forms.

One of the world's most renowned thinkers, Albert Einstein, said something to this effect: "Common sense is the collection of prejudices acquired by the age of eighteen." If Einstein is correct, then your "common sense" has already been affected by the prejudices of society. Therefore, in order to consider any new information that your biased mind might automatically reject, it will be VERY important for you to become like a little child. In other words, instead of rejecting new information that can't pass through the mental filters that have been established in your mind, you must set aside the "collection of prejudices" that you have "acquired by age eighteen." Einstein continued:

> Learn from yesterday, live for today, hope for tomorrow. The important thing is not to stop questioning. ... He who can no longer pause to wonder and stand rapt [absorbed] in awe, is as good as dead; his eyes are closed.

If you do not want to question everything that you know, everything that you have been taught since your early childhood, then this book is NOT for you. If this is the case, perhaps you should end your life if it is not worth living. If you won't open your eyes, then you're "as good as dead" already. But if, for a moment, you can pause to think about and allow your mind to be absorbed in the awe of reading the "marvelous work and a wonder" presented in this book, you will not be disappointed. You will want to live another day.

In living another day, you will begin to see things differently. You will no longer see YOU or your earthly experience through the blindness caused by your "collection of acquired prejudices"—those that have led you to believe that your life is no longer worth living. And then, perhaps, you will want to live an entire lifetime.

The information in this book will give you knowledge that you have never considered before.

However, you must have some *trust* in the book in order to give this information a chance to pass through the hardened filters of your mind.

If you start out with a *hope* that there might be more information that you have never considered before, you will be shown things that you cannot unsee. After reading and contemplating this new information, you will know things that you never knew before. These things will actually make a lot of sense, more than any other information you have ever considered. Knowing these things will *redeem* you from the ignorance that got you to the point of wanting to end your life. Your mind will be opened and enlightened. Then, nothing can stop you from seeing things differently than you will then.

Your parents, peers, teachers, and spiritual leaders may warn you about reading this book. If you are confronted by their discontent and fear of this new information, simply ask them if you should then continue with the choice you are considering: to end your life—a choice caused by the ideas that these people put into your head!

Express to them that all they have done, all they have taught, and all they have counseled did nothing to change your mind. And if they truly cared about helping you make the right decision, why wouldn't they allow you, why wouldn't they even encourage you, to seek knowledge that might save you?

Keep in mind that they are the ones from whom you acquired all the knowledge that is responsible for your common sense. Unfortunately, this "*sense of being*" (your common sense) led you to the point of considering suicide.

Again, it is highly probable that *they* are going to be offended by the new information offered in this book. If they are right, then none of the information in this book is going to change your mind. If they confront you about reading it, plead with them to support you. Explain to them that you want to consider ideas other than what you've received from them—details that promise to help you make the decision to continue living.

Once you have the knowledge provided in this book, you will not see your parents, peers, teachers, therapists, or spiritual leaders in the same *light* as you saw them before. You will understand how ignorant they really were when they were teaching ideas that were *not* how things *really* are. They were not the Real Truth®.

If they have gained value from you looking to *them* to lead you, guide you, and walk beside you, helping you find the way, they will naturally fight this loss by discrediting the information. They will try to convince you that you are being deceived.

However, as explained above, once the Real Truth® is presented to you, and nothing else makes more sense than it does, you will not be able to *unsee* it, or *un-understand* it. No matter how much your loved ones, teachers, and guides "weep, wail, and gnash their teeth" (i.e., become angry), you will not be dissuaded in your continued search to understand things as they *really* are.

The challenge that you must make to your Self is a challenge that led you to consider the Real Truth®. You are reading this information right now for a reason. Challenge yourself to find out <u>for yourself</u> if there is information available that is more logical to your *renewed* common sense. If there is, then you will know that what you learned in the past was *not* things as they *really* are.

_____

As you continue to read this book, you will realize that everyone (excepting those with physical or mental disabilities) has the same ability to learn and understand things as they *really* are, as they *really* were, and as they *really* are to come.

Anything other than a knowledge of how things *really* are, were, and are to come, causes the problems that this world is encountering. Your personal lack of this *real* knowledge has led you to consider ending your life. It can be said that, "whatsoever is more or less than [the Real Truth®] is the spirit of [evil]."

Upon reading this book, you will understand that YOU have the same qualities and abilities to know and understand the Real Truth® as everyone else living upon this earth has. Presidents, popes, priests, and leaders do not have more qualities and abilities than you do. You will be convinced that you do not need anyone else but YOU!

(NOTE: Consider the *quoted* information below that is associated with religious belief.)

The qualities mentioned above can properly be defined as the "*spirit*," or in other words, "those qualities that are regarded as forming the definitive or typical elements of a person, nation, or group, or in the thought and attitudes of a particular period [i.e., spirit]."

The knowledge of Real Truth® ... this *spirit* ... can also be described as "light." This *spirit* or *light* is given equally to every human (with a normal-working brain) that is born upon Earth. In other words, it is "the true light, which lighteth every man that cometh into the world."

We can also refer to the Real Truth® as the "Spirit of truth." This *spirit* will help you to know and understand how the world was created, how the universe was created (if it ever was), and how all things were created by this *spirit*, through this *spirit*, and of this *spirit*, this *spirit* of Real Truth®. Every person living on the earth has a right to receive a fullness of this *light*; or, in other words, to understand all things and know all things (all Real Truth®).

Unfortunately, you have been deceived throughout your life by those in whom you have placed your trust to tell you the *truth* about all things. They have lied to you (most people, unknowingly). Sometimes, they have even admitted that they have *not* "received a fullness of truth, yea, even of all truth." And if they have not, and they admit to that, how can they teach you things, without knowing the truth themselves?

These people whom you have trusted to teach you do not understand how things *really* are. And their pride and ego will not allow them to accept that, without them, YOU ACTUALLY CAN receive a fullness of understanding of everything that did exist, currently exists, and will ever exist.

This book will convince you that YOU CAN "receive truth and light, until [YOU are] glorified in truth and know all things." You will become convinced that you do not need any other person to tell you what to do, what to believe, or how to act.

Upon knowing the Real Truth® of all things, you will understand that YOU are the only God upon which you should depend for this intelligence. You and your brain are the only source and can be the only source of this Real Truth®.

You will find out that YOU "were also in the beginning" with God, as this "*Spirit of truth*," which *is* the proper *intelligence* to know all things; and this "intelligence, or the light of truth, was not created or made, neither indeed can be." It is the same yesterday, today, and forever. (In other words, the real YOU was not created or made and is always the same. It was the same in the past, it's the same in the present, and it will be the same in the future.)

The information in this book will convince you that your life *is* worth living and that YOU are the greatest life form that exists. YOU are the Creator of both heaven and earth and all things. YOU are "the very Eternal Father of heaven and earth." In other words, ALL things relevant to your existence were, are, and will be created in your own mind by exercising free will.

If the information provided in this book saves your life because you found it, considered it, and it made a lot of sense, then it will be proven that YOU are the only savior upon which you can depend. Remember that none of the gods or saviors presented by religion, nor any of their supposed representatives on Earth, could provide you with information that convinced you not to commit suicide.

Having only yourself to depend on, and having the Real Truth® presented to you, your *eternal soul* will gain the power of this intelligence and help you answer the question that you are considering, "To be or not to be?"

If this book fulfills its purpose, you will feel a renewed sense of the importance of your SELF. You will choose to continue this *earth experience*; and continue to be ...

A GOD—THE HIGHEST LIFE FORM POSSIBLE AND THE GREATEST COMPENDIUM OF MATTER THAT EXISTS IN THE UNIVERSE.

Chapter 1

Common Sense

Before you end your existence, think about having your own *Last Supper* like the one illustrated in the famous painting by the visionary Leonardo da Vinci.

If you could invite anyone who currently lives on Earth, or who once lived on Earth, whom would you invite? Keep in mind, these will be the last people living on Earth with whom you will have any type of communication and relationship. After suicide, all communication ends ... and so do all the relationships that you have with other people on Earth. If you commit homicide (kill another person), you end the life of just one individual; but if you commit suicide, you end the life of *all* of the people in your life.

So, you have an important decision to make. What do you want the very last event of your life to be? Because *their words* are the *last* you're going to hear, with whom do you want to share this event? Would you choose the smartest (the wisest) people who have ever lived on Earth? If you did, what would they tell you if they knew this was your personal *Last Supper*?

One of these *wise ones* might say to you, "Please reassess your choice. There is too much recondite information that does not allow any pedagogical fairness in pondering such an existential calamity."

"What?!"

Another might say, "Dude! Nothing makes sense to most of us. Those who claim to have made sense of it all, can't even explain what makes sense!"

The former (the one who spoke first) doesn't seem as amicable (likable) as the latter (the one who spoke last).

What makes you like ... what attracts or endears you to ... another person? Would you rather have people around you who think they have all the answers to everything? Or friends who make you laugh?

The so-called *wise ones* of our world praise and laud (glorify) the works of Socrates and Plato. Another person living during the days of Ancient Greece was *Aristophanes*—a comedian who is mostly unknown. It is reported that Socrates used *wisdom* to confound the pretentiousness (self-importance) and pride of ancient Greek society. Aristophanes used comedy. Both men said basically the same remarks to condemn the leaders of Athens, but one was sentenced to death and the other was applauded and laughed at.

In our modern world, the same irony exists. Comedians get away with making remarks that the audience laughs at during their act. Yet if those same comments were said outside of the theater, it would raise angst and contention with people and potentially cause a lot of anger.

As you contemplate ending your life, consider the people with whom you associate. There are many people who make the decision to end their life because they have not surrounded themselves with people who make them laugh. Instead, they have associated with people who have convinced them that they aren't smart enough ... compared to these others. These others want to carry on a conversation and confront the plethora of recondite information, pedagogically intrusive, that causes an amalgamation of ignorance in the cognitive paradigms that are required by one's existential reality.

"What?!"

If you had surrounded yourself with people who made you laugh every day, would you still be considering ending such an existence of happiness? A popular saying rings true: "Laughter is the best medicine."

There is an obvious difference between the two sets of people presented above. One group acknowledges its ignorance and inability to answer questions about human existence, while the other does everything possible to prove its own value and worth.

More often than not (pretty much always), this latter group makes up ideas and concepts. This group (parents, professors, religious leaders, etc.) uses big words and speaks *intelligently* so as to convince you that its members are smarter than you are. Their goal, in pursuit of their own personal value and worth, is to convince you that what *they think they know* is the *only* truth and the way to achieve success or salvation.

So, you listen to *their* explanations of things (*their truth*). They use every means to convince you that they know what they are talking about (especially when it condemns your personal choices that make you happy). As a result, you become confused.

But you don't want to appear confused. You don't want to appear ignorant and uneducated. If you appear ignorant, you lose value in the eyes of the group who "knows not, and knows not that they know not." The more your personal worth is diminished and devalued, the less meaningful your life seems to be.

Humans are a unique life form that possess a characteristic that no other life form, found anywhere in the universe, enjoys. Humans have a _sense of humor._ This _sense_ is related to the human desire to find and experience joy (_happiness_ being the _expression of joy_). Another _sense_ that is unique to human existence is our _common sense._

If understood correctly, even if scientifically studied with integrity, these two unique _human senses_ could be considered the same thing. One quote states, "Common sense and a sense of humor are the same thing, moving at different speeds. A sense of humor is just common sense, dancing." (Clive James)

The more a comedian relates material that makes sense to the audience, to which the crowd relates and identifies, the more the spectators react with light-hearted laughter. People respond with their _sense of humor_ because of their _common sense._

Why is it then, that Aristophanes was accepted, creating joy for his audience, but Socrates was condemned, tried, and convicted for saying the exact same ideas? The difference was in how the audience _perceived_ the information. When a person attends a comedy show, their mind is open and ready to receive whatever is presented, and their emotional anticipation (expectation) is to _feel_ happiness. Their mind is open (receptive) to the positive feeling because they're expecting it.

The religious and political leaders of Athens were upset when Socrates condemned their political and religious beliefs. This was because of the negative emotional response of the *people*, who gave the leaders their power and value in society. Aristophanes could condemn the leaders all day long and not be a threat to the leaders ... as long as he kept the information confined to the realm of the people's expectations of *comedy*.

It was *common sense* that threatened the status quo of the existing powers that be. Everyone who heard the information understood it, and actually agreed with its presentation. But understanding it versus accepting it as *truth* are two very different emotional aspects of the human mind. In the ancient city of Athens, there was no law that prohibited a comedian from speaking against a politician or religious leader in a theatrical venue. But there *were* laws that prohibited people in general from speaking negatively about their leaders. It was the same truth— the same information. But there was a difference in how the information was delivered and received.

The difference was in how the *rewards* and *punishments* were associated with the delivery. Because there were no laws prohibiting a comedic delivery (full of jokes), there was no punishment. With no punishment attached, a comedian received a *reward* associated with the delivery of the information: laughter. On the street in public though, there were laws; and each law had its own punishment affixed to it. Obeying the law of the land does *not* offer a person any obvious reward, except for *not being punished* for violating the law.

What does the above have to do with your contemplation to consider suicide? Obviously, if you end your life, you're going to receive a punishment or a reward that is related to the outcome of your decision. The outcome, as far as most people on earth believe, is a *punishment.*

Is death a punishment? Or could it be a reward?

Socrates had a choice between death and being exiled. He chose death. Could this be because he considered being exiled to be a *punishment,* whereas death would be his *reward* for standing up for what he believed to be true? Why would Socrates make such a decision? Why would being exiled be more of a punishment than death? Socrates left no personal writings. Therefore, it would be hard for one to determine *why* he made the choice that he did, *rewarding* himself with death.

Socrates chose to commit suicide ... just as you're considering doing. For Socrates, being exiled to another country and continuing to exist among another group of people who were just as ignorant as the citizens of Athens would have been a true punishment to him. His death, however, guaranteed that he would no longer have to associate with ignorant people, who would not use their *common sense* and *sense of humor* to create joy in their lives. From what a couple of disciples of Socrates later reported about his teachings, it is not known whether Socrates believed in life after death or not. His choice to commit suicide instead of continuing to live speaks volumes about the personal struggle he was experiencing while living on Earth.

YOU are as smart as Socrates or any other philosopher. If you feel you are not, why not? What has convinced you to believe that YOU are not? Furthermore, what has persuaded you to believe that your life might not be worth living? Socrates could have chosen to be exiled, rather than to die. You, too, have that choice. In today's world, you can actually "exile" *yourself* to another part of the country or the world and find an entirely different group of people with which to have new associations. Why not choose exile over suicide?

Why not invite the funniest people you have known throughout your life to your *Last Supper*? These people made you laugh before. Maybe they can make you laugh again. By inviting these people to the presumed last event in your life, perhaps you will be *rewarded* by their presence. Perhaps it will lead to your happiness, contentment, and choice to continue living.

The other people, who think they are wiser and know more than you do, present a possibility of a *punishment*. Whether that punishment is that you won't feel as smart as they are, or that they will try to convince you that *you are wrong* for making the choice to end your existence, it's still a *punishment*, and certainly not a *reward*.

In the next two chapters, you are going to have information presented to you that no other author or group of people currently living on this earth knows or can offer to you. The information in these chapters will present answers to the human questions: *"Who are we?"* and *"Why do we exist?"* These answers have never been given before with such soundness, logic, and probability.

The information offered to you in this book is associated with a group of people. If you had the opportunity to meet with this group of people ... with us ... if you chose to invite *us* to your *Last Supper*, you would not be disappointed in what you could learn from us. You would find that our *common sense* supports your *common sense*, causing your *sense of humor* to respond in a very positive way.

You would also discover that there is no *reward* or *punishment* associated with the Real Truth® about who YOU are and why YOU exist. However, all the information you have received during your entire life has been based on *reward* and *punishment*. Therefore, we are not confident that your mind is altogether capable of considering the Real Truth®.

The purpose of this chapter is to convince you to set aside the pattern of *reward* and *punishment* that has been associated with all you have learned since being born into this world. We are asking you to become as a little child again, or you will not be able to receive the information that we are about to give you.

You know how it went when you were a little child. Whatever your parents (or those whom your parents forced you to accept as your leaders and teachers) said was the truth, you either accepted it as such, or you were punished. (You may recognize some punishments as being spanked, grounded, getting detention, rejection, or abandonment, receiving bad grades, getting kicked out, or being failed, for example.) Few parents, if any, counsel their child to figure things out for themselves.

As a little child, the one word that was the most spoken, out of all the new words that you were learning, was: "Why?"

"Why is this? Why is that? Why? Why? Why?"

Your inquisitive (curious) mind often annoyed your parents. And because your parents couldn't answer all of your questions, you felt their frustration and discomfort. This was the *punishment* for your questions. No little child wants to disappoint their parent. Moreover, the parent's *reward* of love, acceptance, and value comes from the little child accepting and believing anything and everything their parent explains to them.

What were your parents supposed to do when you asked a question that they couldn't answer? Their value and relevance were largely dependent on being able to answer your questions ... wanting you to believe, respect, and accept them as the smartest humans on Earth.

The other part of your parent's worth and value was in providing you with the basic necessities of life that your natural physical body craved. You were often *rewarded* when you did something that was agreeable to your parent. That ice cream cone had all to do with your parent providing you with a *reward* for good behavior ... according to *their* rules. The spanking, isolation, and anger and frustration in their facial expressions, were their *punishments* for "bad" behavior—even at times when you may have felt you didn't deserve it.

Because of the way you were raised by your parents, your little mind began to develop a way of accepting and ignoring information that you encountered in your childhood environment. Now that you are grown, if there is not a *reward* or a *punishment* associated with the information that comes into your mind—your brain (being conditioned in this way since birth) doesn't know how to deal with the *new* information; but you can learn.

44

It is known that the human brain is not <u>fully</u> developed until about the age of 25. You learned *how to learn* before that, as your brain was developing. If no one taught you *how* to learn new things, outside of a *reward/punishment* pedagogical paradigm (learning process), your brain will have a very hard time learning any *new* thing.

Consider why you are contemplating the question of whether to be or not to be. You're questioning your existence because of how you *feel.* Because all humans pursue joy (happiness), and you're not finding any in your personal pursuit, you are now questioning whether the pursuit is worthwhile. It certainly doesn't feel worthwhile if you're not finding any happiness!

When you were a little child, wasn't your ability to find and experience happiness a lot greater than it is as an adult? What changed since you were a child? What changed were the *rewards* and *punishments* associated with your experience.

As an adult, no other adult can put you in "time out" (unless you break an adult law that has a punishment affixed to it). YOU are responsible for your own upkeep. You are not going to punish yourself by withholding food and pleasure. However, as an adult who is now responsible for your own food and pleasure, sometimes you might perceive that you are being punished when you do not have enough food to eat or enough opportunity to experience pleasure.

Why is it that there are a lot of people who are experiencing the same world that you are, yet they are not contemplating ending their experience? What is the difference between you and them? Why do they seem to be able to accept the way things are, and not feel that their life is worthless? You're going to be surprised at the answer.

The answer is that these many others are accepting the *rewards* and *punishments* that life hands them ... just like they did when they were little children. These people are awarded for accepting *truths* that come with a reward. One example, using a religious idea, is: "God wants you to do 'such and such' and He will bless you; if you don't, God will punish you." Society also has standards and rules that can reward or punish you, depending on your personally acquired beliefs and acceptance of these standards and rules.

Your dilemma comes from you not accepting *their truths* because these *truths* are not bringing you any happiness. When you question *their undisputed truths*, you are usually punished in some way. Being punished adds to your dilemma. In pursuit of your own personal happiness, in trying to find out a different answer than what is provided by the rest of the world, your life begins to appear meaningless. If humans exist to have joy, and you're not finding any joy, then the natural emotional response to this is that it is impossible for you to find the joy that everyone else appears to be experiencing.

If other people were truly honest with you, they would tell you that they also experience misery a lot more often than they experience joy. But because they don't question the fact that experiencing misery is part of the *earth experience* that no one can do anything about, they don't consider ending their experience. But their reasoning is much more than this.

Again, most people associate *rewards* and *punishments* with their existence as human beings. However, as little children we did *not* naturally accept any restrictions placed on our pursuit of happiness. Instead, we were *taught* (by a reward/punishment teaching method) to accept these restrictions by adults who had been conditioned to accept them.

Now you're wanting to end your life. Have you not been *dining* with the *same* people most of your life? Are these the ones with whom you want to have at your *Last Supper*? Would gathering around your family and friends (parents, siblings, children, teachers, professors, girlfriend/boyfriend, partner, wife/husband, team, coach, religious instructors) be something that would bring you joy and change your mind? Obviously, your involvement with them hasn't done much to convince you to "Keep on keeping on."

Above we wrote, "Why do they seem to be able to accept the way things are, and not feel that their life is worthless? You're going to be surprised at the answer."

These people do not know the information that you're about to learn in the next two chapters. When you consider this new information, you will find that it makes more sense than any other information you have ever considered. If you attempt to share the information with those with whom you have been *dining* your entire life, they will not be able to disregard it because of their own *common sense*. (In other words, the information will make too much sense to them.) As a result, they will probably fight the information. This is because of the *reward* and *punishment* with which they have been indoctrinated, and which keeps them from questioning the status

47

quo. This is the only way they know how to consider new information ... or not.

You've finished this chapter. In so doing and continuing on to the next chapter, you are inviting us to dine with you at your own *Last Supper*. You won't be disappointed with the *feast* we have prepared and placed before you. Our only request is that you consider yourself as a little child. Eat as much as you want, knowing that you will not feel full, no matter how much you eat. And if you eat too much, you will not be punished with an upset stomach.

Except you become like a little child, you can in nowise eat the *fruit of the tree* of Real Truth® about *who you really are and why you really exist*. We have already picked this fruit and are ready to offer it to you. It is a fruit that is most sweet, above all that you have ever tasted before. It will fill your soul with exceedingly great joy. As you eat it, you might begin to be desirous that your family partake of it also; for you will know that it is desirable above all other fruit.

However, don't be surprised if those with whom you have been *dining* your entire life remain in an attitude of mocking you and pointing their fingers at you. Don't be alarmed if they condemn you with punishments that they fear *they* will experience if they *eat of the same fruit* (i.e., if they read and believe the words of this book). Heed them not. In other words, don't listen to them. When they point their fingers of scorn, rely on your *sense of humor* and just smile, remembering that you invited us to your *Last Supper*. You did not invite them.

Enjoy.

Chapter 2

Who YOU Are

The most important thing to understand about who you are is that YOU are the greatest life form that exists anywhere in the universe. There is no life form—a compendium (collection) of matter held together by the power of a universal energy—above, below, in front of, or behind YOU. Regardless of how many other life forms there are, YOU are the greatest.

Your personal existence is the way that you, and only you, experience a *personal* conscious reality. In relation *to* your personal existence, the universe and everything in it is all about YOU. Sure, there are many other life forms, and many other humans. But in regards to your life—your conscious experience—none is greater or more important than YOU are.

According to science, the *Big Bang* theory is the process by which all things had their start. Its spouse is called the *Theory of Evolution*—the process by which all things exist. Giving science its due respect as it searches for ultimate and definitive answers, IF both THEORIES were true, then they would verify that YOU are the best result that came from this marriage of creation. Try to find another life form, or any other thing, as important to YOU as YOU. You will not. Whatever started the process of creating YOU, and however that process might have proceeded, it ended up CREATING YOU.

One might argue that even if you didn't exist, the universe and all other things still would. But to YOU, why would it matter if anything else existed? It wouldn't. If YOU didn't exist, you wouldn't take note of any other thing's existence, nor would you care anything about it.

But YOU do exist. Everything else that exists is only important to your existence to the degree that it supports YOUR existence.

Your *common sense* should uphold and verify the clear facts stated above about YOU and your existence. But it also should remind you that all other human beings are just as important as YOU. In fact, in *their* experience, in *their reality*, THEY are the most important life form that the marriage of the *Big Bang* and *Evolution* produced.

As siblings from this "marriage," in order for members of this *creation family* to get along with each other, each member must understand two things: 1) the importance of the individual Self, and 2) the importance of how each member affects the existence of the whole *family*—the existence of all things. Herein is the human dilemma that we face while going through a conscious experience on this earth, in this solar system.

Humanity will never survive unless the societies that sustain our existence establish law and order based on the following two important principles about human existence—who we are:

> First, love yourself with all your heart, and with all your soul, and with all your mind; and the second is like unto it, you should love your neighbor as yourself. On these two commandments, all the law and order should be based.

Our problems began when some people put themselves above the rest of us, or tried to. They tried to convince us that *they* were more special and should be loved differently than the rest of us. To bring *their Self* more value and purpose, it was advantageous for them to change the first part of these two great commandments, so that the rest of us would love *them* more than we do our own *Selves*.

They created a god who demanded to be worshipped, honored, and loved above anyone and all else. Then they claimed that God had chosen *them* as special siblings in our universal family unit, through whom God gave direction to the rest of us. This placed the control over society in *their* hands.

The human world in this solar system is progressively getting worse. It will continue to get worse until the two commandments above (about how a human should see their self and their neighbor) are properly implemented. These commandments must be applied to the laws that govern us. We must allow the power and control (through law and order) to maintain a consistent harmony of "one heart and one mind, where there are no poor among us."

Currently, there is no *moral compass* that is guiding humanity in the right direction.

Our problems exist because no one seems to know who we *really* are, and why we *really* exist. The next chapter will deal with *why* we exist. This one will explain *who we really are*.

In brief, humans are compendiums (collections) of matter held together by an unseen force of energy that permeates throughout the universe. There is no space in the universe where this energy does not exist. No matter how and when this energy began to form life and all things associated with existence, the human form eventually evolved into, or rather, came to be, what it is: the greatest compendium of matter.

We can use our *common sense* to admit, and hopefully accept, that the human form is the most advanced. We see no other life form that continues to evolve to a more advanced and complex *form*.

In this chapter, we hope to provide you with enough empirical (evidentiary) information to convince you of two things:

1. YOU are the greatest possible life form in your own existence.
2. All other humans are the greatest possible life form in their own existence as well.

Additionally, YOU were formed and are held together by a universal energy that cannot be created or destroyed. This *energy* is the *soul* of a human being.

This energy remains constant and consistent throughout the universe. It always operates by the same processes and protocol to accomplish certain objectives. For instance, when a particular *thing* is created, the process by which it is created is the same throughout the universe. This is because the *energy* by which the process had the power to be performed is the same throughout the universe.

There is a process currently on this earth that uses this universal energy to create the Internet (World Wide Web), as well as *the Cloud* by which a lot of technology operates. Information can be uploaded and downloaded to this *Cloud.* The same energy that is used to upload information is also used to download it. For this process of distributing information to take place, the energy to do so must be present, as well as the *hardware* that was created to perform certain tasks.

The energy that powers the Internet is the same energy that powers the rest of the universe. But left alone, without any manipulation by a human being, the energy would do nothing, not able to act by itself or for itself. It would just sit there and exist. Humans invent and construct *things* to serve *their* needs. (*Servers* are well named and identified as the hardware necessary to host software and infrastructure that allow *the Cloud* to exist.)

Although the following is going to be difficult to accept, it is the Real Truth® about who each of us is as a human being:

Our physical body is the *hardware,* the *server,* that uploads, downloads, and stores energy in the form of consciousness and experience. Without a physical body, our *True Self*—the energy of our *eternal soul*—does nothing but sit there and exist. All it does is wait for some other *thing* (some other compendium of matter) to act upon it. When some other *thing* does act upon the energy of our *eternal soul,* this action allows it to perform the process of giving each of us consciousness and the free will to act and be acted upon.

We hope the information given in this chapter will help you understand and accept this important Real Truth® about YOU.

From our current experience, we know one thing for sure: without humans creating humans, new humans would not and could not exist. By the end of this chapter, it is our hope that you will begin to realize just how important humans are in the universe. And more importantly, we hope you will understand how important YOU are, not only to your own experience, but also to the experience of other people.

Go ahead and ask one of the search engines or artificial intelligence (AI) chatbots the question: "Who are humans?" You'll get many different answers—some scientific and some religious. But you'll get no answers that were the same yesterday, as they are today, and as they will remain in the future.

Keep in mind that the *only* way to have a fair chance at understanding who you are, so you can better determine if you should end your existence or not, is through the Real Truth®. Only Real Truth® can help you. Again, the Real Truth® is defined as things as they *really* are, as they *really* were in the past, and as they will always be in the future. Real Truth® never changes ... ever!

Over a decade ago, AI chatbots didn't exist. If you would have entered the question, "What is human reality?" into one of the main search engines at that time, a link to *Human Reality—Who We Are and Why We Exist* (a book that our group wrote anonymously) would have been the number one hit out of millions. (Please note that this book and *all* other books we have written are available to download FREE on the Internet.)

We wrote this book in an effort to get people to think differently about their own reality. We did not write it with pride or superiority. Our aim was not to cause others to feel less than us. Likewise, we did not want to confuse them by contradicting their traditional religious beliefs. In this 2009 book, we presented information that we believed people could handle and maybe accept and incorporate into their lives.

As human intelligence increases, humans attempt to set a *moral compass* for themselves based on this intelligence. *Intelligence*, however, is different from *knowledge*. Knowledge means knowing some "*thing*." Intelligence is how we use the *thing* that we know.

We wrote the *Human Reality* book more than a decade ago. Science and technological advancements are increasing exponentially at a rate never before experienced. It was our hope in writing this book that, by introducing the correct moral compass, humanity would better itself. Our hope was not realized. Instead, humanity has only gotten worse. Suicide appears to be the *intelligence* (the use of knowledge) that many more people are leaning towards.

We know the Real Truth® is difficult to find and accept in a world filled with strong opinions—each person believing that *their truth* is the only truth, and that everyone else's truth is a conspiracy theory or propaganda. We recognize the failure of humanity to embrace new ideas that often contradict and defeat many established truths (*their truths*). Therefore, in writing and publishing some of the books that we did, we focused our efforts on providing evidence of how orthodox beliefs became unquestionable ("divine") truths. These deceptions have been and are being used to create all kinds of *moral compasses*, none of which have led humanity along the correct path. It is our hope that we can establish a moral compass that can actually help humanity.

Religion is responsible for the majority of *intelligence*—how people use the knowledge they receive from their religious beliefs to construct different moral compasses. Therefore, we wrote and published a book about the *true history of religion*. This book gave a lot of information (knowledge) that is hard for a religious person to accept.

We followed this book with a second book that proved how we attempted to use religion to create a new moral compass that we felt could help save humanity. We explained and provided details and proof of how we created a new American scripture in the early 19th century. This was our attempt to influence the establishment and development of the newly created United States of America.

When relying on Internet searches and AI chatbots, one is exposed *only* to the information that someone else entered into a database, or in another way uploaded to the World Wide Web. Let's suppose that the Internet and AI were available 500 years ago. What if the only information that was *allowed* to be entered or uploaded about who humans are and how they came to be, came from the Judeo/Christian/Islamic Old Testament?

In this scenario, although there might have been ... and there was ... a lot of other information about who humans were and how they came to be, *only* the information from the Bible would have been legal and available (accessible) on the World Wide Web. If this were the case, then no matter how hard you searched for understanding, you would have only learned (acquired the knowledge) that the human race started with two white people—Adam and Eve. According to the *prevailing truths* of that time period, there were no humans before God "created man, male and female created He them." There would have been no other option for discovering truth. *Their truth* would have been the *only* truth.

During this same time period, if you searched the Internet to find out whether the earth was round or flat, you would have only found whatever misinformation had been uploaded to the Internet, which was controlled by law. Your options would have been greatly limited at that time.

Today, your options are many. There are many, many different answers that you can find about who we are and how we came to be. But you must accept that the information you find came from someone who uploaded it to the Internet. It is, therefore, most likely biased towards *that person's truth*, which makes it highly probable that it is *not* the Real Truth®.

A person who does not *know* things as they *really* are relies completely on their understanding of things they learn from others (who don't know things *as things really* are either). If this misinformation is "uploaded" into their brain ... by whatever means ... it is suspect of not *really* being true. The modern *Wikipedia* website provides a good example of this. It allows information to be uploaded, edited, and changed by people. All of these people depend on *their own accepted truths* as the source of the information that *Wikipedia* presents as "facts" for the rest of humanity.

If no one *knew* how things *really are*, then how would it be possible for anyone else to *learn* how things *really are*? What would be the source? As explained above, ALL available sources, if they are created by humans, are suspect of being false and misleading.

If you want to know how things *really are*, the source that you can trust is certainly *not* another person. The source of understanding how *things really are* can only be *how things really are*. You must stop considering any opinion, idea, or information that does not come from your own personal experience. If you have never seen a ghost, then, until you do, ghosts do not exist. If you do not see another life form evolving into a better and stronger form of life, then *evolution* does not exist. You must depend on your own mind and the faculties of learning provided by your senses. "Believe nothing that you hear or read; and only half of what you see."

To make it simple, throw out everything that entered your mind since the time you could remember that you were thinking on your own. Trust no source of information. Begin again. Be born again with a new life and a completely different perspective about what is *truth* and what is not. Create your own truth. Become your own prophet. Become your own god.

It doesn't matter how much learning takes place or how much knowledge humans *think* they possess. This knowledge is going to change one day when someone else comes up with a better idea that makes more sense, and uploads it to the Internet. This changing knowledge cannot be relied on in order to extract the necessary *intelligence* that humanity needs to establish the proper moral compass.

As explained above, humanity is failing because of its inability to first, create the proper moral compass, and then second, unite together as one heart and one mind to follow it. A flawed compass will not, and cannot, guide us to the destination at which we desire to arrive. This destination is and always will be: to experience happiness. Again, in order to understand who we are as human beings, we need only to look at *who we really are.*

Consider a concept that the so-called "wise" and "prudent" ones are teaching; this concept is often referred to as the *SINGULARITY.* Many believe that the integration of, and reliance on, artificial intelligence will one day lead to humans and machines combining together so as to make it difficult to tell where a human starts and a machine ends.

Consider AI chatbots. A human enters a question and a machine answers it. What the machine answers can become this human's reality, or rather, the only *truth* this person will accept. When the human repeats the answer to another human, the person receiving the information does not know its source. The receiver does not know if the answer came from the other person's (giver's) own knowledge, or from the machine's.

In the near future, unless you are sitting right in front of a person and hear the vibrations come out of their voice box and enter your ears, you might not actually be speaking with the person. Avatars can be created to mimic anyone. With advanced technology, even if you are sitting next to a person and listening to what is coming out of their mouth, you will have no idea if their brain is being fed the information from an implant that is linked to the *Internet Cloud*.

For instance, you might not know if you are being "catfished" when you're interested in an intimate relationship with a companion. Who are you *really* communicating with when you text, send an email, converse in a chatroom, or even when you call someone's phone?

This idea of the *Singularity* is not too far-fetched. However, who was it that defined this term in the first place? The person who defined the term *Singularity* as the indistinguishable attributes between humans and machines, stole the term from someone else. Ironically, the first definition of the *Singularity* is actually closer to the Real Truth®—things as they really are—than the lie told by the impostor.

Physicist Albert Einstein proposed a *theory* that a space-time *singularity* is the point where the gravitational field and density of a celestial body (a mass) becomes infinite and cannot be described on a coordinate system. In other words, the point of *Singularity* is when things no longer change, when nothing can act upon it, and it stops acting. It's when things in the past are exactly like they are in the present, and as they always will be in the future. (Sound familiar?)

The energy that created a black hole is considered the same energy that created all matter. *Dark matter* can be considered the *universal womb* in which all things develop into what these things become. But a black hole is also considered the place of death for all matter. The *theory* of a black hole proposes that energy is so strong and focused at a particular point, that nothing can exist in it. The other *theory* that goes along with that of a black hole is the *Big Bang theory*, which attempts to describe how all matter was created.

A *theory* is *not things as they really are*. Theories are suppositions (guesses), ideas, and opinions—all relatable knowledge that makes as much sense as the wisest human can make of it. From these theories, an eternal law of nature was conceived: the *Law of Conservation of Energy*. It is within this eternal, non-changing (the same yesterday, today, and forever) information that humans can find the Real Truth® about who they are.

The Law of Conservation of Energy states that energy cannot be created or destroyed; it can only be transformed from one form of energy to another. This means that a system, or rather a mass of substance (which includes the human body), always has the same amount of energy, unless it's added to from the outside.

A man we spoke with while writing and publishing a new Christian scripture for the American people (as mentioned above), quoted what he had learned about the existence of human beings. Although he was misquoted by other unscrupulous religious leaders (who would lose value because of the Real Truth®), what he said was profound.

This man was a religious leader who knew things about science that no one else at that time knew. However, he could only teach people according to their willingness to accept what he taught. His followers were Christians who believed in the Bible stories about Christ. This man knew there was no god, nor any other entity of energy, outside of one's own mind. However, his followers' acceptance of the Bible's description of Jesus Christ allowed him a way (based on Christian belief) to present information that otherwise would have been rejected outright.

He wrote words similar to what science now understands as the *Law of Conservation of Energy*. Before science published its findings about this eternal law, this man correlated the energy that is responsible for all matter, to the existence and being of God. He knew that all things, including humans, consist of the same source of energy (what science refers to as "protons, neutrons, and electrons"—the basic components of all matter). To his Christian audience, he wrote:

> The light and the Redeemer of the world; the Spirit of [Real] truth, who came into the world, because the world was made by [this Spirit of truth], and in [this energy] was the life of men and the light of men. The worlds were made by [this energy]; men were made by [this energy], and through [this energy], and of [this energy].
>
> ... Ye were also in the beginning with the Father; that which is Spirit, even the Spirit of truth [the same energy of which the "light of the world" exists]; And [Real] truth is knowledge of things as they are, and as they were, and as they are to come.

... Man was also in the beginning with God. Intelligence, or the light of truth, was not created or made, neither indeed can be.

This religious leader tried to help his followers understand that, like their god (Christ), they were "the light of truth," and were "not created or made, neither indeed can be."

The exact same year that science first discovered and published the Law of Conservation of Energy (1842), this man produced a play in which he presented mortal people as sleeping gods. In his play, the character who played the *God Michael* was put to sleep. He dreamed that he was the *man Adam* living upon the earth in a "fallen" state.

This play was called "an endowment from on high." Its last scene demonstrated the mortal man Adam being awakened from the sleep (dream) of mortal existence and becoming again the *God Michael*, whom he had always been. This *God Michael* was not created by another god, but existed equally with all other gods from the beginning. (The original ending of this play was removed later, by corrupt leaders.)

The energy that is responsible for all *things*, including human beings, has always existed the same and will never change. This energy cannot be seen. It *is* what is found throughout the universe and known by science as *dark matter*. This energy can be changed into different forms of matter, but it cannot be destroyed. It is responsible for the system that makes you YOU. It is responsible for the existence of the atoms of the elements that create the molecules of your body and of your brain.

Upon this earth, we cannot see this energy, we cannot feel this energy, we cannot hear, taste, or touch this energy, UNLESS or UNTIL some other thing acts upon it. We see this energy in the form of light and heat (static electricity) when we move across a carpeted floor, or get out from underneath freshly dried sheets.

Although this energy cannot be destroyed, it is responsible for the makeup of ALL things (all things are created from [out of] it). And there is only one life form found anywhere in the universe that has the capacity and intelligence to control and use this energy to create *things*: human beings. If intelligence of how to use this energy comes only from a human being acting upon it, or using it to act, then HOW it is used DOES CHANGE according to the desire and need of the human being.

Therefore, the *use* of this energy is *not ETERNAL.* The way that humans use this energy today was not the same way they used it in the past; and it will not be the same way they will use it in the future. However, regardless of *how* this universal energy was used in the past, is used today, and will be used in the future, the energy itself never changes. It is the same yesterday, today, and forever ... worlds without end.

Regardless of *how* humans use this energy, not even they can create it or destroy it. However, if they use this energy to create some *thing*, then it follows that they can also destroy what they created. Well was it said by an unknowing parent, "I brought you into this world and I can take you out!" This is things as they *really are*.

But what about your *soul*? If your mortal parents didn't create your soul, then it follows that they cannot destroy it. But whoever *did* create your soul (*if* someone did), can also destroy it.

The Real Truth® is, your soul was not created, and neither can it be destroyed. Your soul was not *created* from the energy that has always existed in this world, and in this universe, BECAUSE IT **IS** THIS ENERGY. No matter what your parents or creators do to the body that *they* each created, they cannot destroy your *eternal soul*. However, your *soul* cannot act upon the energy of the universe without a body of mass that allows it to. The aforementioned religious leader told his followers:

> For man is spirit [this energy]. The elements [that come from this energy] are eternal, and spirit and element, inseparably connected, receive a fulness of joy; And when separated, man cannot receive a fulness of joy.

Above, we wrote:

> Humanity is failing because of its inability to first, create the proper moral compass, and then second, unite together as one heart and one mind to follow it. A flawed compass will not, and cannot, guide us to the destination at which we desire to arrive. **This destination is and always will be: to experience happiness**. (Emphasis added.)

65

The next chapter will explain *why we exist*. This explanation must be based on experiencing happiness, because there's no other reason *why* we exist as humans.

You're considering suicide because you have not found happiness. You have given up hope that finding happiness is possible. But who is *really* to blame for your inability to find happiness IF you have been provided with a "flawed compass [that] will not guide [you] to the destination at which [you] desire to arrive" (i.e., happiness)? Did *you* create the body that you possess on this earth? Did YOU give your parent permission to build a body for you? Would you have given your parent permission to make a flawed body for you—one that was not beautiful, not strong, or not mentally capable of meeting the world's standards of value and success?

As we previously explained, your parent follows a flawed moral compass because they don't have access to a proper compass either, nor to the information necessary to *build* the proper compass. Your parent only had the limited information available to them at the time they created your body.

The question remains, however, could your earthly parent *force* the *energy of your eternal soul* to connect with the body that *they created*? When you understand the Real Truth® about who you are, there is no way that you will be able to blame your parent(s) for forcing you to accept the body that they created in their ignorance.

It's easy to blame others for your inability to find happiness in this world. And many times, the blame is justified. Ignorant parents, who do not have the proper *intelligence*, can't do much to provide you with the appropriate compass—one that will lead you and guide you to happiness throughout your mortal existence.

When you die, you will continue to be conscious as a thinking, feeling compendium of matter, in a body. Your *eternal soul* requires a body in order for YOU to continue to think and exist as a conscious human being. If this is true (and it is), then who created *this* body? Could it be that the creator of your pre-mortal and post-mortal body had the intelligence necessary to create a body that *would* allow you to always experience happiness? The only way that another person could do this, is if this other person is much more advanced and much more intelligent than your parent(s) on Earth is (are).

Your mortal parent has no idea about the energy of the universe from which they were created. No matter how sincere their search for an understanding of how things *really are*, they have only had other Earth people from whom to get their answers. It doesn't matter how sophisticated and advanced their search engines and AI chatbots were. If no one was uploading the Real Truth®, it would have been impossible for them to find it. Without this information, how could they ever be expected to create a correct body for YOU—one that would allow you to experience happiness?

Your mortal parent(s) has/have an excuse for not helping you find happiness. Their excuse is that they don't know the Real Truth® about human existence. But they are justified because they did *not* force you to connect to the body that they created upon Earth, no matter how flawed the body was.

Your soul is made of the same material (energy) as the rest of the universe. Therefore, whatever happens to this *energy* ... to YOU ... affects all bodies of mass that are connected to this *energy*, in the same manner that it affects YOU. If a piece of matter existing in one part of the universe is affected by some *thing*, everything else in the universe is affected at the same time and in the same way. It is important to keep in mind that there is no existence of any *thing* unless something else causes its existence.

There is no *space or time* associated with the *energy* that exists in the universe and connects and affects all matter.

Let's suppose you live in a galaxy that is trillions of light years away from the Milky Way Galaxy. When you sneeze, anyone, living anywhere else in the universe, could—if they chose to—see, hear, taste, smell, and touch your personal sneeze in real time.

There is NO MASS (matter) OF ANY KIND that is not connected to the human experience. Every light that you see at night has something to do with humans. Every sun that exists was created by humans who had the intelligence to create a new sun. This is why the universe appears to be expanding. Around each sun, advanced humans can create whatever planet (mass of matter) they desire for their happiness, if they know how to.

The *Law of Conservation* states that "a system always has the same amount of energy, unless it's added to from the outside." A sun and its planets constitute a *solar* *system*. There was once just potential energy in that part of the universe. When "that system" had energy added to it, it changed the system. The creation of a sun does not destroy energy. It creates new energy from *dark matter* (the energy from which it was created). (In the Introduction of this book, we explained the Real Truth® about *gravity* and *magnetism* ... things as they *really* are—what science has yet to call a *law* instead of just a *theory*.)

The energy of the universe was not created and cannot be destroyed. Your *soul*—the energy that allows you to think and be conscious—is, was, and will always be part of the universe. However, in order to be YOU, a body of element (mass) had to be created by some other body that had the intelligence to do so. This leads to the question about who or what created the first creator. If nothing can exist without some other *thing* creating it, then what created the *thing* that did the creating? It is this question that plagues the minds of humans who do not know the Real Truth® about their own existence. "If God created men, then who created God?"

The answer to this question is so simple and so easy that it is often discounted because of its simplicity. The Real Truth® is this:

There has *never* been a *time* or a *space* where human beings have not existed ... in one form or another.

The elements are eternal and exist throughout the universe in various forms and compendiums that create all the different *things* that exist. Every *thing* has ALWAYS existed in some part of the universe.

Consider the chicken and the egg. Which came first? The answer is simple: neither. They both have always existed somewhere in the universe.

Your flawed (or better, imperfect) mortal brain does not have the capability to fully comprehend that ALL THINGS have ALWAYS EXISTED. And it's not your fault that you have this flawed brain. It's not your fault because, in your search for happiness, your choices of physical bodies were limited to the number of these bodies that other flawed humans had created.

If you decide to go through with your suicide and end the consciousness of your flawed brain in your flawed body, you will immediately realize that YOU actually *do* exist in a perfect body made by other humans who had the proper intelligence to create this perfect body.

The religious leader mentioned above told his followers, "The glory of God is intelligence, or, in other words, light and truth." He taught them that they were gods, equal to the most intelligent humans that could possibly exist. He taught them that, "As God is, man once was. And as God is, man will return to be." Unfortunately, his followers didn't understand him.

Later, corrupt religious leaders hijacked his teachings and altered what he said. Today, these deceptive leaders teach their followers that, "As man now is, God once was; as God now is, man may become." These unscrupulous leaders (a few, sincere) need an invented "God" to take precedence over individuals (to be superior to them) so that they, the leaders, can control society. They define who and what "God" is. Their definitions always include ideas that support their existence as leaders. They always benefit from their invented priesthood authority.

Consider if it were accepted that all people are actually gods themselves, who will return to be a god when their mortal experience has ended (i.e., "As God is, man once was and will return to be"). Then it follows appropriately that all people are their own prophet, seer, and revelator of their personal god's will. This is the Real Truth® about who you are and why you exist. And so why should we put our faith in any man, "whose breath is in his nostrils"? Why not have faith in ourselves?

A man who cherishes his power and authority over others (as well as the value and worth associated with his "calling" as a prophet, seer, and revelator) wants his followers to ignore him as a man, focusing on the belief that one day he will be a god. However, when this man dies and returns to be the god who he has always been, whatever this man has done while on the earth, ends and becomes of no worth when he dies. This Real Truth® affects a religious leader's ability to maintain their power and control over others, and the value of their position in doing so.

Once this person dies, they will return to be the same human they were *before* they connected to an imperfect mortal body. At that time, they will lose all the value and worth they accumulated while experiencing life upon Earth, while teaching people the falsehoods that gave them their own personal worth. As our good book said, "It would be better for them if they had not been born." Maybe it isn't YOU who should be considering suicide. Perhaps it

71

should be those who have wielded power and authority over you. But that is up to *them*.

Hopefully in understanding *why you exist*, the pieces of the puzzle will begin to fall into place and prove to you just how incredibly important YOU are to the entire universe!

Chapter 3

Why YOU Exist

In other chapters, we will explore more about *who you are* and *how* you exist. The previous chapter was basically an introduction that summarized who you are.

Humans are the greatest life form (compendium of matter) that can possibly exist in the universe. Humans are the most important life form that exists. All other life forms exist to serve human need. This "need" is to experience what humans recognize as joy (happiness being the physical expression of this joy). As individuals, each of us is the greatest of all life forms ... at the very least, in regards to our own existence.

It is hard to challenge the above summation of who we are based on our first-hand, physical senses (what we see, hear, smell, taste, and touch). Our common sense—our sense of reality, speaks to its truth. Living day to day upon the earth, the empirical evidence of our (human) dominance over all other forms of life, or other forms of *any* matter, is indisputable.

Some would argue that the natural world does not need humans in order to exist. In fact, some might argue that the earth would do better if we *didn't* exist. But if we didn't exist, why would it matter how well the natural world was doing? To whom or to what would it matter? We are the only life form that makes a constant effort to utilize all other forms of matter for our benefit. What these other forms of matter might feel or believe about the way that we use them does not change our efforts. No other life form *feels* like we do. And none has the capacity to *believe*.

You are considering suicide, ending your existence as a life form upon Earth. What would it matter to the natural world, or to the rest of us, *if* you did? Sure, there are a few people who might mourn your non-existence. And if you are a popular, well-known, and well-liked person, there might be many who would mourn your loss. But your fans wouldn't be sad about the *real* (genuine and authentic) *you* who no longer existed. They would only be sad about the loss of the person whom *they* wanted you to be. They really don't know YOU, do they? They only know the person you pretend to be, to please them, so they will like you.

Furthermore, if you are a popular, rich, well-liked person, why would you commit suicide? You're popular, well-liked, and have all the money you need—to do anything that you want to do while alive on Earth. Why would you end your existence? You might commit suicide because you realize that no one *really* values you for the person who you are behind the acting, outside of the performance, and under the mask you put on in order to be loved by them. You know that the person *they* love doesn't really exist. You know they would not love you if you did *not* act and perform behind the mask that you created *for them*—a persona that was created not for YOU, but for them!

Why did you become something for *them*, losing your *true* and *genuine identity* in the process? When you were a very little child, did you act, perform, and wear a mask? No. But as you grew, you began to realize that others had an expectation of you that gave *them* joy, even when you knew it wasn't who you *really* were. You were then backed into a social corner. You had a decision to make: "Do I stay true to myself and be lonely because nobody likes the *real me*? Or do I become whatever it is that *they* want me to become, so *they* will be happy?"

You're forced to weigh the options between loneliness or the companionship of others. As little children, we sometimes forced our individuality on *others*. However, when what we wanted for ourselves wasn't what others wanted us to be *for them*, we were punished. We were punished for being true to ourself. We learned that our existence was not really *only* about who we were as an individual, but also about how our presence caused others to experience *their own* happiness. The more we brought happiness to them, the more loved, the more valued, and the more accepted we were *by them*. But why?

As stated above, all other life forms exist to serve our individual need. This "need" is to experience what each of us feels as joy (happiness being the physical expression of this joy). Therefore, all of us are doing the exact same thing—pursuing our individual happiness. We use "all other life forms," which include *all other people,* to experience this joy. We "need" other life forms, especially ones similar to us, in order to experience this joy.

Those upon whom you depend for happiness, also depend on you for *their* happiness, in the same way and for the same reasons (for value and acceptance). So, the struggle begins ... we want *them* to be the way that *we need* them to be for *our* personal happiness, and they want *us* to be the way that *they need* us to be for *their* personal happiness.

What if you were *really* created, not for anyone else's happiness, but *only* for your own? What if your creator didn't have any expectations for your happiness because they were already very happy and fulfilled? What if they didn't need anyone else to exist or do things to bring *themselves* happiness?

Did our earthly creators create us for US? Or did they create us for THEM?

There are two simple differences between the human species and the rest of the animal kingdom—*self-awareness* and the *ability to reason*. This ability is not instinctual and did not come from years of cognitive evolution, as some would suggest. From scientific speculations, the **myth** of "cavemen" was formulated. It was theorized that their grunts and groans eventually developed into a communal language of cooperation, which aided in the success of the species. If this were the case, science would see the same development in other animal species. But it does not, and will not. This is because these other species don't have the ability to reason. Also, they are not aware of the *self* as an individual part of a greater whole, possessing the ability to exercise free will in order to maintain *their* individuality.

This self-awareness and the ability to reason can appropriately be called "selfishness." We (humans) are the only purely selfish creatures in nature. After our basic needs of food and procreative sex are met, our selfishness motivates us to eat for pleasure, have sex for pleasure, and further establish our individuality from the rest of the whole of humanity. Therefore, "selfishness" becomes a natural human tendency by reason of our own existence. Recognizing "selfishness" for what it truly is establishes a positive definition instead of the negative connotation generally recognized as improper behavior.

The individual is the essence of the *Homo sapiens* (wise ones). For us to find this "essence," we must experience a lifetime of choices acting contrary to the whole, in order to maintain a balance of self-awareness and individuality. We divide ourselves into family units to develop and maintain individuality. A male and female do not commit to lifelong partnerships to contribute to the whole, but to maintain self-awareness.

"Love" is a value placed on something outside of the self. Being "in love" is a selfish abstract human creation. We "love" someone if it contributes to our individuality. When we no longer feel support from our partner, "love" no longer exists. For example, a woman will stay "in love" with a man as long as she feels the man sees her as his "one and only," the most beautiful example of womanhood, or any other emotional support that builds her self-perception that she is uniquely distinguished from other women.

We may also form partnerships with those of the same sex, with no intent to procreate, but to maintain the essence of our individuality. When a male, for example, senses he is valued by another male, even though his individual preference does not fit the accepted "norm," the union is emotionally justified.

This is because it appears natural and appropriate to both men whose individuality is supported by it.

Our parents did not consciously desire us (their children) to guarantee the perpetuation of the species. Instead, we were created to give more credibility and support to them. Our father and mother validated themselves by creating us. Most family rules and expectations are not set to allow us (their children) to become individuals, but instead, to further their *self*ish desires, in order to maintain their own individuality.

As we grow up, we eventually become aware that our existence is no longer dependent on our parent(s). Our *self* becomes more important to *us* than the whole of the family; thus, a rebellion ensues. This ultimately brings heartache and instability to our family unit, which was not instituted for our sake, but for our parents' sake.

To further maintain the purpose for which we exist—to find and experience joy—we have placed values on other abstractions that can more easily establish our individuality. Material possessions become a distinction of class and prestige (houses, cars, jewelry, toys). Distinctions of the accumulation of knowledge (not intelligence) set us apart from others, allowing our self-worth to foundationalize individuality. A college degree or employment experience that none other has achieved helps us maintain this value of our *self*. The color and style of our hair, the jewelry adorning our body, and other personalized choices support us as an individual against the whole.

Self-awareness creates our individual human experience, and the ability to reason maintains it. These unique human characteristics determine the balance by which we acquire a personal awareness of our *self.* If maintained properly, this balance serves us well, and gives meaning and purpose to our existence.

Individuality is the value placed upon our existence. When this value is compromised, there is no longer balance. Humans recognize balance and imbalance as happiness and unhappiness respectively.

Like "love," "happiness" and "unhappiness" are abstract emotions felt when we receive, or don't receive, recognition for our uniqueness. When we are not acknowledged separately from the whole, the purpose of our existence is breeched, and we become unbalanced, contrary to our nature. Either we exist in a continual state of unhappiness, or we seek to alleviate the discomfort by setting ourself apart from the whole, thus fulfilling the measure of our creation.

We seek to fulfill the purpose for which we exist, which is to be recognized and valued as individuals in our search for happiness. Because of this, we use our superior intelligence over all other life forms to accomplish this goal. Because our goal is individual and has nothing to do with the whole of humanity, whatever or whoever interferes with reaching this goal becomes a detriment to our happiness (balance).

One thing is certain about our existence as human beings: we could not have existed without another human being becoming involved in our existence ... in our creation. Although the energy responsible for the existence and support of our *eternal soul* is everywhere and in every *thing* that exists throughout the universe, we cannot have an individual *conscious* experience without someone ... another human ... creating a physical body to which the *energy of our soul* can connect (either an advanced body or a mortal body).

Energy cannot act upon itself to create a *thing*. It is impossible. It remains energy until it is acted upon by some other force of energy and told what to do. Again, energy cannot act on itself, despite what some scientists visualize occurring with the *Big Bang*. Scientists cannot explain *how* or *why* this event occurred. They can only *theorize* that it did. This is because it makes sense according to their limited understanding. It might make sense to their imagination, but when asked to show an example of this in our *real* world, science cannot find one.

Consider crude oil that lies beneath the surface of the earth. It cannot do anything until some other thing acts upon it. This organically created material has existed for billions of years ... as far as science knows. During that time, what life form, other than a human, saw oil and acted upon it to serve its needs? NONE.

Consider nuclear energy. This *energy* exists in every *thing*, because every *thing* has a nucleus that uses this energy to make whatever the *thing* is. This nuclear energy is found in ALL things throughout the universe. If science wants to try to convince us that *nothing* was responsible for acting upon this energy in order to create the *Big Bang*, it becomes a scientific duty to show us an example of this. But science cannot show us any example of this happening naturally.

Nuclear explosions do not happen unless humans make them happen. It wasn't a chimpanzee that figured out how to use oil and nuclear energy to serve its purpose for existence. Animals existed for millions of years without figuring out how to use oil and nuclear energy. However, within the last 100 years, humans have been able to figure it all out *and* start using these resources to assist them in their pursuit of happiness. Humans discovered these things because they are the *only* life form that has *self-awareness* and the *ability to reason*.

In the previous chapter about who you are, it was explained that *all things* have *always existed*, and that there was never a time when *nothing* existed. If you were to travel throughout the universe and go as far as possible, you would find that it is impossible to reach an end, because the universe is never-ending. No matter how far you were to travel, you would run into worlds without end.

Let's suppose that you have a powerful telescope aimed at a particular point in the universe. Yesterday, there was no point of light in view. But today, there is. Let's say that, instead of *theorizing* about why there is a point of light today that wasn't there yesterday, you jump into a spaceship and go to investigate. What would you find?

Keep in mind that we don't want to use our imagination, or we could have just as easily peered into the telescope and invented all kinds of *theories* and speculations of why a new light appeared where there was once none. To know the Real Truth®, you have to go there and see, hear, smell, taste, and touch the event for yourself.

Let's say you leave our earth, traveling to a point of light (solar system) that is billions of light years away. On this earth you have just traveled to, you find humans who have figured out how to utilize the process of fusion to create a new sun out in space. They have done this so it is far enough away from their current sun so as not to impede on or affect their existing sun's operations. You show up on their earth and ask, "What's going on?"

Their response to you is, "Well, we figured out how fusion works and how to create a new sun. We used science and mathematics to calculate where we had to go and how far we had to travel, in order to set off a fusion explosion in space to create a new sun."

"Why did you need to create a new sun?" you (the alien visitor) ask.

"Because we could," they respond.

You, the alien to this earth, look around this world and find out that their civilization is much more advanced than your own. They have learned how to eliminate aging, sickness, disease, and all the other factors that can end a person's life without their individual permission. You can see that the people of this earth have figured out how to live peacefully with each other. They don't have borders. They don't have money. Everyone has everything and anything that they want and need, as long as their private possessions do not impede the ability of another person to have the same possessions, if it's in the best interests and happiness of the other person.

You find that the government of this planet and its power and laws are based on serving the needs of the individual, equitably and with equality. Because these people have learned how to cooperate so well with each other, they were able to learn how universal energy works on the quantum level, and how it can be used for human need. They can create anything they want, simply by a chemical process that they control. Everything they do benefits every human equitably ... not the same (equally), but impartially and fairly.

You see that there are young people among them. But you realize that none of them is gendered. You find out that the people of this earth learned how to create new human bodies asexually (without using sex). You see how incredibly wonderful these bodies are. You notice they took all things into consideration when designing these human bodies so that, in the creation of one, it did not take anything away from the current existence of another. They are the *perfect human physical bodies*.

Then you ask these people about their history and this is what they say:

"Many years ago ... a *lot* of years ago ... human bodies were created sexually by people who wanted a child, not for the sake of a new human *soul*, but for the sake of the parent. Our history reports that these bodies were created specifically to serve their parents ... their creators. These types of bodies caused a lot of the new children to experience misery, because they could not find their own happiness in serving their parents' needs for their existence."

They continue, "When DNA from a parent was used, it was done so that the newly created body would serve the purpose and existence of the body from which its blueprint was taken. When new bodies were produced sexually, two different people passed on part of their *own* identity to form another person. They also passed on their personal desires for happiness. Often, the two parents were very different in their personal desires for happiness. This conflict between the two parents' personal identities caused confusion for the newly created person. When the two parents passed on the blueprints of their life experiences, in hopes that their child would add to their *own* happiness, the parents' different pursuits (desires) of happiness created chaos and confusion in the new child's mind.

"In our distant past … many, many years ago in our history … we figured out that you don't need to use another person's DNA (the blueprint of their existence) in order to create another person. We found that the children who were the products of the two-parent reproductive process couldn't find their own individual happiness; and many—most—killed each other and themselves to end the turmoil. It became apparent to us that, if we wanted new human beings to join our human society on this planet, we needed to help these new people continue to exist without wanting to kill themselves. Thus, we developed a new way (our current way) of creating physical bodies.

"None of our current bodies … those living in this perfect advanced world … have any connection with anyone else's body. DNA, the blueprints provided by people who had a hard time finding their own happiness, was not passed on to us. We learned how to create new bodies that allowed a person to pursue this newly created person's *own* desires of happiness—not from the expectations and natural enticements of the parents, but of their own making. When we started creating bodies in this way, the expectations of the newly created person's happiness were COMPLETELY and UNCOMPROMISINGLY based on the new life experiences of the newly created person.

"We have had very few, if any, problems since creating these types of human bodies. The only problems we have encountered happened when a few of these newly created—completely independent of any DNA expectation—bodies lived for a lot of years, developing their own sense of happiness. As they did, their individual pursuit of happiness began to cause some uncomfortableness for the rest of us. This was not because they were judged as being odd or abnormal in their individual pursuit of happiness, but because our perfect world could no longer provide them with any new experiences for which these people longed.

"So, because these people are just as important as the rest of us, we thought it best to create a new solar system where these few could experience a different society that *they*, and *they alone*, created for themselves. We figured that, if they had this experience, they would then realize why they were making the rest of us feel uncomfortable."

"Oh," says you (the alien), "that's why you created a new sun. You wanted to give others the opportunity to live in a different society that wasn't perfect. You knew this opportunity might allow your children to engage in their own unique pursuit of happiness, thereby experiencing what *your* ancestors did when they decided to change things that led to your now-perfect society."

You continue, "I see the new solar system off in the distance there in space. But where are the spaceships that will carry these people to this new world?"

"We don't travel in spaceships," they reply. "There's no need. We will create new human bodies on the new planets in that solar system just as we created the sun that began that solar system's existence. Once these physical bodies are created, a person living here on our perfect planet will be able to connect the power of their mind to the body there in order to begin the new experience in that solar system."

You ask, "You mean I didn't need a spaceship in order to travel all this way to see what made that new light that I observed through the telescope I was using?"

"Correct," they tell you. "We didn't invite you here. You came on your own, in pursuit of your own curiosity. We can teach you all that you need to know so that you will never need a spaceship to travel to any part of the universe. We can show you how to connect to the *Universal Wi-Fi* that allows all people, living anywhere in the universe, to connect instantly to whichever solar system they desire. Do you play computer games on your planet?"

"Yes," you answer.

They continue, "When you play the game with someone living thousands of miles away from you in another country, on the other side of your world, do you travel there in order to participate in that virtual, wireless, experience?"

"No," you tell them. "But the other players have a computer, like mine at home, by which we can connect to each other and play the game in real time."

They explain, "The same power and energy that allows you to connect to the *wireless* energy that powers your Internet, also allows anyone in this universe to connect anywhere else in this universe in real time. You just need to have the right hardware to connect to this power and then use it appropriately."

"Can you create a physical body for me in this perfect world, so that I won't need a spaceship the next time I want to travel here?" asks you, the alien.

"Yes, we can," they tell you. "But for it all to work properly, you'll have to end your existence on your home planet, because your body was created by the blueprints of two imperfect people. Nothing in the DNA that your parents passed on to you allows for this *Intergalactic wireless connection*."

"So, I'll have to commit suicide there, in order to connect to this perfect world?" you ask.

"Correct. But that's completely up to you," they reply. "However, if you had not visited our perfect world in person, you would not have known that for sure. And you would be taking a chance that there would not be a body created for you yet, for you to continue your existence. Be patient. You are actually just like the newly created children that we created for our perfect world—those for whom we created this other solar system."

They continue, "We understand the problems and complexity of living in your imperfect world. It is our hope that our children will likewise understand when they live in this new solar system that we specifically created to help them learn more about themselves. However, please understand that if you prematurely end your existence in your current *imperfect world*, you will not gain the experience that your *True Self* (living in one of the other perfect worlds out there) wanted you to gain from this imperfect existence.

"Your mortal brain is connected to your actual, advanced brain of your *True Self.* In allowing this experience on Earth to play out, you will realize when you die that, although you 'died,' you're not really dead. It will be your mortal self—that person who you're really not—who will be gone.

"You will then understand *why* you chose to be a mortal person, how important it is, and how impactful it was for your understanding of yourself. Because that's the only thing that matters: yourself.

"YOU and your personal pursuit of joy is the only thing that matters."

Chapter 4

A Life Worth Living

Is your life *really* worth living?

In the previous chapters, we explained that the universe has *always* been. We explained that humans are the greatest life form possible. A life form is any *thing* that exists and acts within and upon the universe, in the sphere in which it was created, to perform the operations and functions for which the *thing* was envisioned and created. A *life form* can only act according to its coding, or rather, according to the instructions that give the *thing* the ability to act and be acted upon by the rest of the *life forms* found in the universe.

We depend on *common sense* to back up this Real Truth®. Without theorizing about what happened in the past, or believing in something that was not experienced by our five senses, we must depend on what we are experiencing today ... IN THE NOW.

There is no empirical (observed) evidence of the present that does not support the Real Truth® that humans are the greatest compendium (collection) of matter that exists. There are many creative guesses that entertain an uneducated and curious mind. Regardless, there is no *thing*, found anywhere in the universe, that functions and operates with a greater capacity and potential (of acting upon and being acted upon in the universe) than a human being ... ABSOLUTELY NONE.

In the previous chapter, we presented a scenario about what human existence in this solar system might be like in the future ... IF the human race on Earth doesn't end up destroying itself. This should have made a lot of (common) sense. We presented the idea of a new human body being created by utilizing higher intelligence and more advanced technology than what is presently (2023) available.

We explained that *sexual* reproduction is very imperfect because the child inherits bad DNA traits, both physically and emotionally, from the two-parent (male and female) process. Non-sexual reproduction of a human life form can be controlled and used to create perfect physical bodies that do not age, get sick, die, or in other ways cause misery to the person.

It makes a lot of (common) sense, in the creation of new physical bodies, to eliminate all the ways that a body can suffer while living in this solar system upon this planet Earth. In our presentation of this Real Truth®, we juxtaposed* this *more perfect* way of creating human bodies to what some of humanity's major religions propose in the Bible. (*This means that we contrasted these two ways so they would cause a powerful cognitive dissonance in a person's mind.)

The Bible does *not* say that God created bodies for Adam and Eve through sex. It *does* say, however, that Eve's body came from Adam's body. This introduces the idea that the male body has the capacity—according to the Bible's story—to create a female body. Furthermore, this popular and accepted narrative presents the idea that sexual reproduction was a *curse* as a result of Adam and Eve's free-willed choice.

It isn't hard for an honest Bible-believer to see the contradiction between the way that the Bible's god created the first humans and the way that modern Bible-believers think humans *should* be created (sexually, by a man and a woman). This cognitive dissonance (mental conflict) holds believers captive to their limited understanding of God's ways and means. It also causes a lot of heartache and misery, because of the arguments and hard hearts of those who do not believe that humans should be created by any other way or means than through the male and female sexual process.

What is a god, if not an entity that has more intelligence than another entity? One quote states, "The glory of God is intelligence, or, in other words, light and truth." *Truth* is things as they were in the past, as they are today, and as they will always be in the future. If we can accept these statements, then modern humans are the gods of the past—at least according to the perception and intelligence of ancient humans, compared to those of the present world. If one could travel back in time and show people living in ancient Greece, for example, a smartphone, and how it performs its operations and functions, this person would be perceived as a god.

The people of today are the gods of yesterday. The people of the future will be the gods of today—where "God" can perform operations and functions that the people of today can only imagine that a "god" can do.

In the previous chapter, we presented a very easy-to-consider scenario about what the human experience might be like in a few thousand years, bearing in mind the current rate that technology is advancing. Keep in mind what "technology" is. *Technology* is simply the way that humans create new *things* to perform operations and functions for which the *thing* was created. All *things* that humans create are usually produced to aid humans in the purpose for which they exist. This purpose is to experience happiness. These human-created *things* are coded and given instructions to allow the *thing* the ability to act and be acted upon by the rest of the *things* found throughout the universe.

As described in the previous chapter, we used crude oil and nuclear energy as two of many examples of what humans can do with other *things* to serve their needs. Another example is electricity. As we explained:

> A life form is any *thing* that exists and acts within and upon the universe, in the sphere in which it was created, to perform the operations and functions for which the *thing* was envisioned and created. A *life form* can only act according to its coding, or rather, according to the instructions that give the *thing* the ability to act and be acted upon by the rest of the *life forms* found in the universe.

Here, we presented the idea that future generations of highly advanced humans will create bodies using extremely developed technology, allowing a *new* person (a new life form) to exist upon the earth. In our hypothetical scenario, we explained:

We have had very few, if any, problems since creating these types of human bodies. The only problems we have encountered happened when a few of these newly created—completely independent of any DNA expectation—bodies lived for a lot of years, developing their own sense of happiness. As they did, their individual pursuit of happiness began to cause some uncomfortableness for the rest of us. This was not because they were judged as being odd or abnormal in their individual pursuit of happiness, but because our perfect world could no longer provide them with any new experiences for which these people longed.

So, because these people are just as important as the rest of us, we thought it best to create a new solar system where these few could experience a different society that *they*, and *they alone*, created for themselves. We figured that if they had this experience, they would then realize why they were making the rest of us feel uncomfortable.

When humans create a *thing* that is coded and preprogrammed to perform certain operations and functions that serve humans, it is highly unlikely—in fact, it is impossible—for the *thing* to do something that causes people to feel uncomfortable. But when one of the codes or programs given to the new *creation* involves self-learning, outside of the parameters set by the primary and principal operations and functions, that *thing* has *free will* and the possibility of doing whatever it wants.

In today's world, as technology advances at an unprecedented speed, some fear that the machines (the *things*) might take on a life of their own and one day dominate and control their creators (us). This, however, is *not* possible when the *thing* is preprogrammed and coded properly. In the future, humans will invent and produce many robots that will serve *human* need. Even if a machine is programmed to learn by itself, it is still impossible for it to learn something outside of the original parameters set for whatever it is that the *thing* was created to do for humans.

In our hypothetical future scenario, the *creators* of the new human bodies wanted to help these *free-willed* life forms to learn, by their own doing, what it is that makes others feel uncomfortable. As explained, this is the reason why a new, different type of solar system was created. (This is the reason why our solar system—in the *Milky Way Galaxy*—was created.) These newly created *things* were not robots. They were human beings. They were specifically created to allow the *new person* to self-learn and do as they please.

A *failsafe* is a mechanism that causes a machine to revert to a safe condition in the event of a breakdown or malfunction. While all robots (machines) created have some type of *failsafe* incorporated into their preprogramming and coding, bodies created to become new human beings do not have any *failsafe*, when and IF they are *properly* made. This is because if they had any failsafe programmed into the operations and functions of the physical body, the person wouldn't have complete *free will*.

Now let's consider a human body that is *improperly* created to produce other human bodies through the sexual, male-female process. There shouldn't be much argument about the purpose for the male's sperm and the female's egg. Let's say that all of the males got together and decided that they no longer wanted to create any new children. The females disagreed, but because of the physical strength of the males, the females couldn't very easily rape the males, forcing them to give children to the females.

These types of human bodies were *created* and *programmed* to reproduce themselves through the sexual process. The creators of these bodies wanted their *creations* to continue to reproduce to fulfill the purpose for which these new bodies were created. Sexual hormones that are *involuntary* and cause a person to lust and want sex were the *failsafe* that was introduced into the creation of these bodies. This was done to make sure that a person's free-willed choice *not* to create a new child would be overridden.

In other words, sexually-based bodies are a mechanism used to ensure that new humans will be created. To the creators of these bodies, continual sexual reproduction was the "safe condition" for which they envisioned and created new human bodies. The presence of strong physical sexual desires, caused by hormones and the experience of an orgasm, fixed the "breakdown or malfunction" of the free-willed person's desire *not* to have any children.

In the hypothetical future of our very advanced world (as described in the last chapter), there were no genders. There were no preprogrammed *failsafes* incorporated into the newly created ... PROPERLY CREATED ... human bodies. Advanced humans, who had learned from their past mistakes, realized that the strong desire to have sex caused an enormous amount of problems in their society.

These advanced humans knew what they were doing when they created new physical bodies. The bodies they created allowed each new person to experience life, not being forced to act or be acted upon in any other way than the way that person chose. This was the only way that the newly created person could pursue their own individual happiness that was not based on someone else's desires of happiness. (As we explained in the last chapter: parents who pass on their DNA also pass on *their desires of happiness, based on their experience.*)

Keep in mind that in this highly advanced world, there is nothing that creates misery for the human experience; everyone is experiencing the same thing—eternal, unrestricted joy. Therefore, *if* these advanced humans passed on their DNA to a child, the child would *not* have any of the experiences that cause human problems passed on to them. But the child would *not* be a free-willed entity (life form). The child would be a creation *for* the advanced parent, and not a creation *for* the child's own, personal development and experience.

The perfect human experience is when one is able to pursue their own individual desires for happiness, whatever those desires might be. A properly created person's DNA is new and unaffected by any other human's experience or desires of happiness. In a perfect world, new humans are created by people who have the newly created person's best interests in mind.

It is impossible for a preprogrammed life form to experience things and develop a sense of individuality through these experiences, *unless* the person can program and code *their own* operations and functions. A good, *perfect* parent/creator is one who recognizes why humans exist.

Again, humans are that they might have joy, not from the happiness they see others experiencing, but from what they do with their *own* free will. In advanced worlds, humans have figured out that anytime a person is forced, in any way, to do something to please another person, or to support *another* person's happiness, the person is *not* pursuing *their own happiness*. In not pursuing one's own happiness, a human brain can never reach the point that causes the person to feel an *eternal sense of joy*.

Our brains are the central warehouse of all our experience, emotions, operations, and functions. Therefore, our individual brain has either been preprogrammed and coded to produce these products, or it has developed its *own* emotions, operations, and functions.

Sexual reproduction passes on the DNA from our parents. This creates a brain that has been developed from blueprints based on *other* people's experiences of happiness (our parent's). Because our brains are currently formed this way, we must pursue operations and functions that meet the criteria of happiness that constructed this "warehouse." If we cannot perform the operations and functions that provided our *parents* with an experience of happiness, we will never find constant joy.

If we had the opportunity to build a "warehouse" of our own creation and invention, we would establish the operations and functions that allow our brain to bring about the products of happiness. These products would not be based on previous experience, but upon the new experiences that we are encountering in the NOW, during our daily life. The "building" could be whatever we want it to be—a unique and personalized manufacturing process that only we oversee and control.

The operations and functions of our parents' manufacturing plants (the physical brain of each) are based on our parents' expectations of what they experienced during their conscious life. For a properly created human being to experience what the brain feels as joy, that person must have a brain that has not been foundationalized (pre-established) with any expectations of this feeling.

To make it clearer, it is not the actual experience that creates joy, but the ability of the experience to meet the expectations placed upon it. These expectations were set while each person's brain was consciously engaged in the environment that was provided for the senses. The senses are the ways and means by which we experience consciousness (sight, touch, smell, taste, and hearing). Sexual reproduction passed our parents' experiences on to us. If we are able to meet the expectations of the parents' experience, then our brain experiences a feeling of balance. This feeling is what we describe as joy.

If no experiences were passed on to us (as they are with sexual reproduction), then we would not have inherited the expectations that were part of these experiences. For example, if a child is given a round rock to play with, and the child has no other experience of playing with a round object embedded in their brain's operations and functions, the child will be just fine playing with the rock. But, if the child's parent was a football (soccer) star, and while playing the game the parent experienced a lot of joy from the applause and praise that came as a result of their athletic ability, kicking a rock around is not going to meet the expectations passed on to the child by their parent who was a star athlete.

The talents of a child prodigy provide evidence of the above. The child has a natural propensity to excel in a field that one of the child's ancestors pursued as the ancestor's experience of happiness. The DNA of the child is a partial blueprint from the ancestor's brain, which always includes the ancestor's experiences of happiness. If the child of the football (soccer) star mentioned above does not have an opportunity in their life to meet the expectations of happiness passed on from the parent, the child will experience an imbalance that emotionally expresses itself as frustration and depression.

In this example, the child might be a great football player, but in the child's *new* experience, there might be many other great football players that compete to fulfill the expectations passed on from these other players' football-experienced parents as well. And those players might be better than the child.

Advanced creators living in highly advanced worlds understand how the inheritance of both physical and emotional traits affect a newly created person. For this reason, they do *not* create any new bodies based on DNA, full of expectations of another time period. The newly created people set their *own* expectations, which are never passed on to any other person.

By allowing a newly created person to pursue their own unique experiences, there's always a possibility that the person is going to have experiences that bring the person happiness, but at the same time, cause others to feel uncomfortable.

For example, let's say that a newly created, advanced human child lives, has experiences, and grows and develops, setting their own expectations and conditions of happiness. Their brain is always balanced because they're the only one in charge of what they do and how they fulfill the expectations that they have for their own happiness. In a lot of cases, though, advanced humans see that other advanced people are experiencing happiness doing things that they do not do, or things that are not part of their own experience. They often wonder if they would experience the same sense of joy as the other person is experiencing, if they did what the other person is doing.

Many newly created, advanced humans wonder, "Would the result for me be the same as it is for them? Would I, too, feel happiness if I did what *they* are doing to experience happiness?" As an example ... and this is just one of many, but it is a good example ... we are going to use one of the strongest human emotional and physical feelings that is *humanly* possible: an orgasm. It's not hard to see the effect that an orgasm has on a person. Any person who has experienced one recognizes that, during the incident, ALL the human senses are enhanced and contribute to the experience.

Remember, in most advanced, perfect human societies, none of the people are gendered. Therefore, none have the physical body parts that are required for an orgasmic experience. However, there *are* solar systems that exist throughout the universe where *everyone* living on the planets in these *specialized* solar systems has the body parts required for the human brain to experience an orgasm. These solar systems are *specialized* because they are the only place where new humans can be created properly. These solar systems are the only place where *human creators* exist. These people have only *one* expectation for their individual happiness: to *properly* create other humans to exist in the universe.

The people living in these specialized solar systems do *not* have free will. At some point in their past experiences, they determined that sacrificing their own free will, in order to follow a precise and established plan and protocol in creating new people, was the *only* expectation that they placed on their existence and happiness. While they are serving as creators, they cannot go anywhere in the universe and do whatever they want. They have chosen to be *creators* and must remain on the planet that allows them to create new humans.

There was a condition for choosing this specialized existence ... and there was also a reward. The condition was that they give up their free will and exercise their position as a *creator* for the sake of the free will of others—in this case, their children. The reward was the ability to experience an orgasm.

Keep in mind that the universe has always been the way that it is, except for the fact that it continues to expand. This is based on new worlds that are created to allow the many new humans to exist and pursue their individual happiness. If there were no new people who wanted to sacrifice their free will to become *creators* of new perfect children, then there would be no expanse of the universe, because there would be no new creation. To motivate a person to give up their own free will for the sake of another's free will, a reward is offered. The ability to have an orgasm anytime is that reward.

So, consider yourself as a newly created, advanced, perfect human. Your first experiences were living in the same solar system as your creator. Once capable and willing, you were able to go anywhere you wanted in the universe, checking things out and seeing what worked and what didn't work for you in providing you with the experience of feeling joy. You saw that your creators were greatly inhibited in their own experience, because they never left their solar system. They didn't have any new experiences, except those that *their children* had and shared with them. You didn't want to be like your creators. That's a boring existence!

Finally, you came across a solar system ... let's say in the *Milky Way Galaxy* ... that seemed to be just right for you. This solar system had other non-gendered advanced people living there who had set expectations similar to what you had set for yourself as you developed throughout the many, many, many years of your existence.

Keep in mind that in order for you to travel to this solar system, that might be trillions and trillions of light years away from your creator's planet, you didn't travel by spaceship. Someone in this chosen solar system had to construct a body to which you could connect the power of your *eternal soul*. These people were *not* creators, however. These people developed bodies that are made specially and specifically for the solar system that they ... and now you ... had chosen, based on their experiences since the time of their creation as a newly created human being.

This body was *not* the body that your creator made for you, and in which you had existed for many, many years, trying to find what expectations of happiness suited you. You understood that the moment you connected to this new world, you would be forced to end your existence on your creator's planet. Yeah, you had to voluntarily, with your own free will, commit suicide on your home-based planet, ending that existence, which also ended the bonds you shared with your creator forever.

Think about it. If this weren't the case, then there would be countless newly created humans living in a *Creator's Solar System*, and no room for anybody new to come into existence.

So you made the choice. Now you existed as a perfect, advanced human being living in a solar system in the *Milky Way Galaxy*. Everything seemed fine at first. As an infant, you started bonding with the adults who helped you learn how to use the body that was specifically designed for this solar system.

You were a young infant child when you first connected to this new solar system ... away from your original creator. But you grew up and became the exact same age, so it appeared, as everyone else living in this solar system. You were able to fulfill all the expectations of happiness that you had developed throughout the time between being created by an actual, gendered *creator*, and now—with a bunch of non-gendered adults living in your chosen solar system who helped you grow and learn the ins and outs of this new world.

So, you became an adult—ungendered and living in the perfect world. You learned all kinds of things about the universe. Although you could not remember your creation, or your original creator, you knew they still existed out there, somewhere else, doing what they would always do: create new human beings ... worlds without end.

You then started talking with a few friends and contemplating the Real Truth® about all things, especially what you knew about your *First State of Existence* ... the one you couldn't remember. You started discussing gender, sex, and the orgasm that would be possible, if only you had a gendered body. You and your friends made others living in your solar system feel uncomfortable. You see, you were a "new" person in this solar system. Most of the people there had been around for a long time. They had already thought about being gendered and being able to have an orgasm; but they weren't bothered about it any longer.

Many of the older ones (based on how long they had lived in this new solar system) explained that they had also once questioned and discussed the same things. They had realized there was only one way they would understand whether they had made the right choice of living in their new solar system (it wasn't new to these *older* ones).

Besides the experience of an orgasm, you began to wonder what it would be like to be a Creator. What would you do with this power? What kinds of plants, animals, and other life forms would you create if you were allowed to live in a world with unconditional free will to basically do what *you* wanted? You wanted to be something that others living in your new solar system didn't care about becoming. You thought that by becoming someone different than who you were as a highly advanced human, you might feel a stronger degree of happiness.

Alternately, maybe you and a few of your friends decided that you really didn't need to be gendered so that you could experience an orgasm. Maybe the group of you just wanted to do something that made you stand out and be more *special*, or at least different from all the other people in your chosen world.

Everyone in your perfect, chosen world had great self-esteem and self-importance. This is an *ego* that all humans have in common. But there is a *common enemy* that cannot be tolerated in any perfect human society. That common enemy is PRIDE.

Pride is different from an ego. All humans have an ego—it's what makes us human. But there are a few who want a "feeling of deep pleasure or satisfaction derived from one's own achievements, the achievements of those with whom one is closely associated, or from qualities or possessions that are widely admired" (the definition of pride).

You and your group of friends thought about achieving things that the other people living in your chosen perfect society weren't achieving. In this way, you started making the other people in your chosen perfect solar system feel uncomfortable. You and your friends didn't understand why, in pursuit of achieving something different than what was possible in your already advanced world, you were making other people feel uncomfortable. It didn't make any sense to you.

The people who were starting to feel uncomfortable with you and your friends weren't upset with you. They were just uncomfortable. Because you were kind of a *newbie* in their world, they realized that you needed some experience to learn what would happen in a world where everyone was seeking a "feeling of deep pleasure or satisfaction derived from one's own achievements, the achievements of those with whom one is closely associated, or from qualities or possessions that are widely admired."

They encouraged you to connect to planet Earth and gain the experience of being *prideful.* (Pride is the common enemy that all advanced human societies have cast out.) By connecting to our current solar system, you would have the opportunity to pursue this *pride.* If, upon living here, you found that pursuing this *pride* actually brought you happiness, then you would realize that the new solar system you had chosen as your *Second State of Existence* wasn't really what you wanted.

So here you are presently on Earth—pursuing this *pride*. But it's not going *your way*. Because everyone else in our world is pursuing the same *pride* ... the same feeling of deep pleasure or satisfaction derived from one's own achievements, the achievements of those with whom one is closely associated, or from qualities or possessions that are widely admired ... you're not happy.

You are not finding any pleasure or satisfaction from your own achievements, or from the achievements of others with whom you are closely associated. You realize that you are *not* widely admired, nor do you have the qualities or possessions that are widely admired by others living on planet Earth. And you are not happy.

You have found that your life is no longer worth living, and you can't seem to find the "deep pleasure or satisfaction" for which you long. You are burdened with the question, "Is my life really worth living?"

Now you have a choice to make: "To be or not to be."

But before you make the choice, there are some other things that you need to know about the *nature of your eternal soul.*

Chapter 5

Fulfilling the Measure of Your Creation

So, why do YOU exist? And will YOU continue to exist after your brain shuts down and your physical body eventually deteriorates back into the elements from which it was formed? We tried to answer these two questions in the previous chapters. These two questions are relevant to your decision to end your life or keep on living. However, we cannot be sure how much of the information we provided to you was accepted by YOU as the Real Truth®.

With regard to the first question, we hope that common sense can help you answer it honestly. You can only answer it according to what YOU know and have experienced as a conscious life form living on Earth. Only your senses can give YOU this experience. Based on this experience, the answer to "Why do YOU exist?" must be: "Because my parents created me."

What you know, then, is that you could *not* have created yourself. In order for any *thing* to exist, some other *thing* that already existed in the universe had to act in order to begin the process of its creation. It logically follows, then, that whoever or whatever created YOU, had their own reasons and purpose. In the case of your earthly parents, it very well could have been that the only reason and purpose for your creation was that your parents were overcome and controlled by their natural sexual desires. Therefore, if their sexual desire and pleasure was the reason, then your creation was *not* a free-willed choice made by your parents.

If your parents didn't *choose* to create you, then who or what else did? Who or what acted upon the universe and the *things* found therein (if anyone or anything actually did), so that YOU could exist?

We hope that we have proven to you that *no thing* exists without some other *thing* making it exist. Even if the Big Bang theory were correct, then some *thing* (other than all the *new things* that the big bang created) acted *first*, setting the event in motion. Science has theorized that the universe and every *thing* found in it, began as just a single point of energy, which then expanded and stretched to grow as large as it is right now; and it is *still* increasing. What science cannot competently answer is, "*WHY*?" Why did this single point of energy (if there was one) start expanding? What was the plan, or course of action, taken to achieve the creation of the universe?

A *measure* is "a plan or course of action taken to achieve a particular purpose." The *measure of creation* of any *thing* is the plan or course of action taken to achieve whatever the *thing* eventually ends up doing. According to scientific speculations, the best it has to offer—the measure of the universe's creation—is to create *things*. What leaves ALL scientists scratching their heads is trying to figure out what the "particular purpose" *was* of the "plan or course of action taken" by the Big Bang. What was intended? If *creation of all things* was the intention (the plan or course of action), then *why* was this measure taken? And who or what took it?

We have tried our best to convince you that you should not accept any theory, speculation, or belief UNLESS YOU can personally experience what is being defined or explained. Based on this litmus test of Real Truth®—things as they *really* are and as they *really* were—humans are the *only* life form that has the ability and intelligence to create *new things*.

We can create new plants. We can create new animals. We can create all kinds of different new bacteria and viruses. And surprisingly, soon, we will be able to create the four basic nucleotides responsible for the DNA involved in the creation of *all living things*. Furthermore, and just as important, we have even created *new elements*. Besides human beings, there is no other life form—that you have personally witnessed through your own senses—that can create *new things* from the eternal and universal elements found throughout the universe.

Science can theorize all it wants about *things*. Religion can have faith, which is the substance (fundamental nature) of *things* hoped for, the evidence of *things* not seen. But neither of these *belief systems* can answer the question of *why* things exist the way that they do. What is the *measure of each thing's creation*?

Religion confuses a person by impeding or stopping (and, more often than not, forbidding) the study and experimentation of creating things. Religion relies on the belief in a god that created all things for God's own purpose. At least science remains open to changing its beliefs, if better evidence is presented.

Science, however, is also based on *faith*. It *hopes* that the evidence of scientific exploration and experimentation is sufficient enough to recommend its *faith* in its scientific methods over religion's blind *faith* in God. Science cannot see energy. Therefore, the substance of scientific theories about energy is based on "the evidence of things not seen."

A *deist* is person who believes that God created the universe and then abandoned it. They hold the opinion that some kind of supernatural force (god) *must* exist though, based on the evidence of *reason* (common sense). A *theist* holds and defends (with a lot of war and misery) that there is just one God. They believe that this God created all things and is still actively engaged in the creation of new things, causing the universe to expand. Many of the most popular scientists were *deists* instead of *theists*. The theist believes that if the Big Bang theory proves to be correct, then it was God who made the bang that set into motion the creation of all things.

As we have pointed out to you, calling upon your common sense and ability to reason, God can't do anything, and is *not* doing anything to convince you to continue to live. Neither does science provide you with much help in making the right decision for YOU. We have tried to convince you that YOU are the only god that exists over YOU! The only way we might be successful at convincing you that our information is the Real Truth® about *all things*, is to do something for YOU that religion and science cannot. We can answer the questions about your existence. We can explain *the measure of your creation*.

Now, whether you believe our answers or not is YOUR prerogative (privilege) and free-willed choice. We cannot force you to accept our information. All we can do is present it to you. If you've gotten this far in this book, then our information has made you curious. Hopefully, we can encourage you to finish this book and consider what we know is the Real Truth® about human existence.

We do not say that our information is going to change your mind about ending your life upon this earth. In fact, we wouldn't blame you if you did. But, again, before you do, consider everything that we present to you as a possibility of how things *really* are. We suppose we are asking you to exercise a bit of *faith* in our information.

In order for you to have any faith, in anything, you must first exercise some *hope*. And what is it that you should hope for? You should hope that there are *real answers*—Real Truth® ... because there are! There has to be! Regardless of scientific or religious opinion, or even of *our* opinion, there can only be ONE way that *things are the way that they are*, and the way that they have always been ... worlds without end.

There is only one answer to the question of whether or not YOU continue to be a conscious *soul* after experiencing a mortal, physical death. There are not two or three answers. There is only one answer, as there has always been and as there will always be.

Perhaps you will still be confused after considering our information. If so, you could easily find out for yourself by committing suicide. But let's consider what you are doing ... based on the information we have presented to you thus far ... in making the free-willed decision to end your existence on this earth.

We have explained that when you die, your mental energy (eternal soul) will continue on in the highly advanced body that YOU chose for your existence in this universe. We have explained that this connection occurred the moment you, as an infant on Earth, took your first breath. This connection caused you, as the infant, to no longer be dependent on your parent (in the mother's womb) for existence. You began to breathe on your own, acting on and being acted upon by the energy provided by Earth's *specific* environment.

To make it easier and much clearer to understand, let's divide the human *state of consciousness* ... where the physical body takes in energy from the environment in which it exists, and also gives off energy back into this environment ... into THREE distinct states.

FIRST ESTATE

During the *First State of Consciousness* ... our *First Estate* ... a body is created so that the process of human existence can begin. This process of human existence is started by allowing the energy found throughout the universe to react with the operations and functions meant for a new *human* brain. The plan or purpose for which this body is created (the *measure of its creation*) is to allow the newly created person to find their own identity and desires of happiness, prodded on gently by our advanced human *creators*. These creators allow *any* free-willed choice, as long as the choice taken by the new person does *not*—in any way,

113

shape, or form—impede another person's free will. We call this process the FOUNDATIONALIZATION OF THE HUMAN SOUL.

The people who create these perfect human bodies in our *First Estate* do nothing more with their own free will (by their own choice) than create new bodies, so that new human beings can exist. They do *not* create these bodies for *their own* desire or pleasure. They create these bodies solely for the *new human being*. These bodies are infantile in nature, so that the newly created person can learn how to use this type of body correctly. Again, this is done with the gentle prodding of an advanced parent.

There is *no* DNA ... blueprint of life ... passed on by these *creators*. Each creator chooses what the body looks like. Each body is made distinct and unique, based on a variety of physical appearances that separate each new person from all of the rest of the newly created people. All new bodies are formed with the most beautiful countenance and features possible.

The body we possess in our *First Estate* is completely and unconditionally free-willed, so long as our choices do not negatively affect the existence of any other person. We can do what we want, when we want, and how we want. However, this is always under the guidance of our highly advanced parent.

After existing in our *First Estate* for a very, very, very long time, we develop our own unique individuality. This foundationalization process provides us with the power to temporarily connect (virtually) to any solar system that exists anywhere in the universe. We briefly (compared to eternity) connect to many, many different advanced worlds, trying to find one that fulfills the *measure of our creation as an advanced human life form*.

The *measure* for which we were created and given life was to experience happiness. This happiness is based on our unique, individual experiences, developing under the subtle and gentle tutelage of the creator who gave us life.

Once we figure out what makes us happy and find a solar system with people of similar desires of happiness, we want to join with these people. We want to become a living, conscious human being existing on a planet, in a solar system, where our expectations of happiness can be fulfilled. Upon finding this new solar system, we must disconnect the energy of our *eternal soul* from the body created for us in the *First Estate*, so that we can be fully conscious and 100% connected to the new experience.

SECOND ESTATE

Whereas our *First Estate* can be considered the home of the God who gave us life, our *Second Estate* is the new life, new relationships, and new home we choose for ourselves. Our creator is not going to kick us out of *their home*, off of *their planet*. We have to make this choice by ourselves. The hardest part about making this choice is that we cannot keep the body that was created for us by our creator. The body we had in our *First Estate* was created from the same elements that created the solar system that houses the planet upon which our creator continues to create other humans.

Yes. We had to make the decision to commit suicide. We would not have made this decision if we didn't know for sure that our new experience would continue to fulfill the *measure of our creation*—which again, was to experience joy through the expectations that we established for ourselves during our time in the *First Estate*. During the *Second State of Consciousness* ... our *Second Estate* ... a body is created of the same materials from which a new advanced solar system was created.

Keep in mind, there are no spaceships that transport humans between galaxies and solar systems. A new physical body was made of the same elements from which our chosen solar system was made. This was carried out by someone else currently residing on the planet upon which we wanted to start a new experience of living. Once this body was formed, only then did you end your physical existence in the *First Estate*, so that you could exist in the *Second*.

We've explained that this connection occurs by way of an *Intergalactic Internet Cloud* ... for want of a better way to explain it ... that allows a real time connection no matter where you might be living in the universe. But you cannot have two actual physical bodies at the same time. Moving forward, your *True Self* resides in the *Second Estate*.

Our mortal bodies on Earth create dreams as part of our brain's operations and performances. Similar to this, our *True Self's* brain has the ability to have *dream experiences* that seem very real while we are having them, but are *not* the physical

116

experiences of our *True Self.* Our existence upon this earth can be considered a *dream of mortal life*.

Again, YOU ... the eternal YOU that YOU control—that has no beginning and no end, UNLESS YOU end it—can only exist in one body with one brain. Mortal life on this earth, however, can be considered the *Third State of Existence*.

THIRD ESTATE

During this *Third State of Consciousness* ... our *Third Estate* ... a virtual body is created inside the mind (the brain) of our *Second Estate's body*. This is just like we exist in our dreams that are experienced subconsciously on Earth while we are asleep. (The dreams that we experience while living on this earth can be considered a *Fourth State of Consciousness* ... our *Fourth Estate*.)

Our mortal life on this earth is a conscious experience that is generated by and in our physical brain in the *Second Estate*. This process of connecting *temporarily* with another solar system is the exact same process that we used to connect to many, many different galaxies and solar systems as we were developing our expectations of experience and happiness in our *First Estate*. Again, there are no spaceships that transport human beings from one solar system or galaxy to another. There is no need.

The difference between our *Third Estate* and our *Fourth Estate* (a mortal *dream state*) is that the solar system where planet Earth exists is an actual, physical place that can be observed from anywhere else in the universe. Conversely, neither we (when we are not dreaming) nor our friends, can see the world in which our mortal dreams take place. Furthermore, only YOU alone have these experiences in a *dream world* (*Fourth Estate*). If we've made friends during our time in the *Second Estate*, they are welcome to join us in connecting to planet Earth in our *Third Estate*, partaking of the life experiences provided here.

In the previous chapter, we explained the *measure of your creation* as a human mortal living on this earth. We presented this information by describing your free-willed desires. We wrote:

> You wanted to be something that others living in your new solar system didn't care about becoming. You thought that by becoming someone different than who you were as a highly advanced human, you might feel a stronger degree of happiness.

We explained that you might have a group of your friends in the *Second Estate* with the same desire. We wrote:

> Maybe the group of you just wanted to do something that made you stand out and be more *special*, or at least different from all the other people in your chosen world.

We explained the difference between the *ego*—something that ALL humans living throughout the universe have in common—and PRIDE, which no advanced society allows. We explained that "everyone in your perfect, chosen world had great self-esteem and self-importance" (i.e., EGO), but YOU and your friends desired a "feeling of deep pleasure or satisfaction derived from one's own achievements, the achievements of those with whom one is closely associated, or from qualities or possessions that are widely admired." You wanted to feel PRIDEFUL of your own existence.

So, now you find yourself miserable in the *Third State of Existence* (mortal life) because you are *not fulfilling the measure of your creation*. You are meeting resistance from everyone else who also chose to come to this earth for an experience. The "plan or course of action" that you, and everyone else who lives on this earth, chose, had a *particular purpose*.

Again, a *measure* is a "plan or course of action taken to achieve a particular purpose." Your plan or course of action was to achieve personal or group PRIDE. You and your friends wanted to experience a "feeling of deep pleasure or satisfaction derived from one's own achievements, the achievements of those with whom one is closely associated, or from qualities or possessions that are widely admired."

You are *not fulfilling the measure of your creation*, which is the plan or course of action that you intended for yourself. Keep in mind that every advanced human who lives on the same planet in the same solar system with you in the *Second Estate* chose, as you did, to live there for their eternal existence to pursue their personal happiness. *Most* of the other advanced humans living there did *not* and do *not* want to connect to this earth. They chose *not* to partake of this

"Tree of Knowledge of Good and Evil" (the enticements of the mortal flesh) of planet Earth.

These others did *not* desire to experience what it was like to feel PRIDEFUL of their existence. True, there *are* some who have already tried out the experience of PRIDE. And just as you are finding out for yourself, these people found that it was *impossible* to experience constant happiness in a world where people are seeking a feeling of deep pleasure or satisfaction derived from their own achievements, from the achievements of those with whom they are closely associated, or from the qualities or possessions that are widely admired by others.

This PRIDE is a "common enemy" that is cast out of every successful advanced human society ... EVERY ONE.

You might want to end this mortal dream experience because you, obviously, are not feeling a deep pleasure or satisfaction derived from your own accomplishments. You are *not* fulfilling the measure for which you were created as a mortal living upon this earth.

And now, here's the most important question that only YOU can answer: If you *were* experiencing a feeling of deep satisfaction derived from the *earth experience*, would you want to end your life? Would you be happy in experiencing this PRIDE? If you *were* happy living a *prideful* (pride-driven) life, then you *would be* fulfilling the measure for which you came to this earth. You came to experience this PRIDE. Upon experiencing it, you may have found happiness in the experience. But you have forgotten a VERY important thing about this PRIDE.

THIS PRIDE DOES NOT EXIST IN ANY ADVANCED HUMAN WORLD. NO SUCCESSFUL HUMAN SOCIETY TOLERATES PEOPLE WHO SEEK FOR A FEELING OF DEEP SATISFACTION DERIVED FROM THEIR OWN PERSONAL ACCOMPLISHMENTS OR ACHIEVEMENTS, THE ACHIEVEMENTS OF THOSE WITH WHOM THESE PEOPLE ARE CLOSELY ASSOCIATED, OR FROM THE QUALITIES OR POSSESSIONS THAT ARE WIDELY ADMIRED BY OTHERS.

No advanced human being ... ABSOLUTELY NONE ... cares about what you might achieve in your own pursuit of happiness. They are only concerned about their own happiness. No advanced human gets a "feeling of deep pleasure or satisfaction" because of something that another advanced human might achieve. They simply don't care.

And if YOU care that they don't care—and because you're not able to achieve these feelings (which you now have proven to yourself bring YOU "deep pleasure and satisfaction,")—the rest of the people living in the *Second Estate* are going to do the only thing they can. They must act so that they do not have to feel uncomfortable. They are going to cast YOU out!

So, now how do you feel about committing suicide and ending your existence? Why do you want to? Why are you so unhappy?

In the next chapter, we will review the many ways that people living on this earth are able to feel a deep pleasure or satisfaction derived from their own achievements, the achievements of those with whom they are closely associated, or from qualities or possessions that are widely admired by others. We will further explain this PRIDE, and why this loftiness of ego is destroying our world, like the other worlds it has destroyed. You will then understand that you can either choose another plan or course of action (a new *measure of creation*) for your existence, that doesn't include *pride-filled* (prideful) intentions, or you can end your existence now.

Upon ending your existence because your *pride* was hurt or threatened, you are ending, or greatly limiting, your chance of learning that WHO YOU WANT TO BE is NOT someone who YOU *REALLY* WANT TO BE ... worlds without end. The most important question that only YOU can answer honestly for yourself is:

What is the measure of YOUR creation?

Chapter 6

A Lone and Dreary World

In previous chapters, we described two different ways that humans express their emotional need to be recognized as an individual and as part of a group: *ego* and *pride*.

We explained that all humans possess an ego, regardless of the degree of their advanced (living in the most advanced worlds) or underdeveloped (living in worlds of a primitive nature) *state of consciousness*. Our *ego* is a feeling of self-esteem and importance that is primarily based on how we value ourselves. It is established on our own opinions and beliefs about ourselves. Our egos are a natural product of our existence in any given environment (advanced or underdeveloped). On the other hand, our *pride* is based on the opinions and beliefs that others have of us.

In our *First Estate*, we did not have a free-willed choice to exist. Advanced creators made a body and a brain for us that could connect to the universal elements responsible for all consciousness. Referring to our *Second State of Existence*, which is a world you did choose for yourself, we wrote:

> Everyone in your perfect, chosen world [*Second Estate*] had great self-esteem and self-importance. This is an *ego* that all humans have in common. But there is a *common*

enemy that cannot be tolerated in any perfect human society. That common enemy is PRIDE.

Pride is different than an ego. All humans have an ego—it's what makes us human. But there are a few who want [to feel this *pride*, which is] a 'feeling of deep pleasure or satisfaction derived from one's own achievements, the achievements of those with whom one is closely associated, or from qualities or possessions that are widely admired.'

There has never been a world, located in *any* solar system, found *anywhere* in the universe, where humanity survived for any significant period of time when the inhabitants of this world had PRIDE. (Prideful people always seek recognition from others for their own achievements, or for the achievements of a group to which they belong, or from qualities or possessions that are widely admired by the world in which they exist.) In every case, humans ended up destroying themselves because of PRIDE.

One need only be honest about what is recorded as the history of humanity for the last ten thousand years upon this earth. No society, no matter how great and expansive, has lasted for more than about 1000 years. In each and every case, PRIDE was the culprit (reason).

The downfall of human society begins when one person wants to be recognized for their own achievements. Each individual who needs this *recognition* requires the support of a group of people with the same goals and desires to do the *recognizing*. It is from this group that the person seeking pride in their accomplishments can gain the platitudes (thanks and appreciation) they desire.

However, the moment that one group encounters another group that does not agree with the first group's goals and purpose, wars ensue, and people are killed. More often than not, *all* of the people of one group are killed by the stronger group.

When the mass members of these groups see the power and wealth of just a few individual members, the majority begins to question the minority's specialness. The few are recognized by the masses for their achievements. This meets the definition of pride. Again, this definition is when the members feel a deep pleasure or satisfaction derived from the minority's achievements (those of "the few"), which gives the majority the same sense of pleasure or satisfaction. In almost every case, "the few," who become the leaders of the group, are admired by the other members of the group for their qualities and possessions. (Some examples include basketball players, movie stars, politicians, and religious leaders.)

No group can remain cohesive and successful unless it has *few* leaders and lots of followers. If there are too many leaders and not enough followers, the group is quick to fail. Throughout history, when the leaders of the weaker groups realized they were about to fall to a stronger group, they retreated and led their followers outside of the boundaries that the stronger group created for itself.

Having lost members to war and death, the weaker group often left and found another place to live, but they continued to hate their conquerors. The weaker group would then wait for a time when they could regroup, become stronger, and attack their conquerors. In this way, they would get reparations and return to their original homeland.

In ancient times, there were no means of communication or other ways that the many groups of humans would know about other groups. This is because the earth is a large place and there were many different groups existing throughout the world. This is how nations, languages, cultures, traditions, religions, and customs developed among the different groups scattered throughout the earth. These differences and divisions developed because the groups of people needed a way to continue to *feel* a deep pleasure or satisfaction derived from their own achievements.

Borders, nations, languages, cultures, traditions, religions, and customs allowed the people to *feel pride* for the achievements of their particular group. Likewise, these divisions provided opportunities to *feel pride* from qualities or possessions that are widely admired, not only by any one group, but by all the rest of the other groups too.

As *pride* spread throughout the societies of humans living on Earth, it seemed as if there existed an unseen, powerful entity that threatened to disrupt peace and harmony among humans:

> I will take the treasures of the earth, and with gold and silver I will buy up armies and navies, popes and priests, and reign with blood and horror on the earth!

Keep in mind, although divided by borders, nations, languages, cultures, traditions, religions, and customs, *all* groups desired gold and silver. All treasured *money*. Money is an abstract value placed on possessions that are widely admired by *all* groups. If one group has more money than other groups, this one group usually comes out on top as the stronger group.

There is an "enmity" that exists in the human mind. We are inspired by our egos to believe and hold the opinion that our self-value and importance is just as appreciated and important as everyone else's is. This antagonistic (unfriendly) feeling, this *enmity*, supports what each of us feels inside: "I am just as important as anyone else in this world."

In Chapter Two, *Who You Are*, we wrote:

Humanity will never survive unless the societies that sustain our existence establish law and order based on the following two important principles about human existence—who we are:

First, love yourself with all your heart, and with all your soul, and with all your mind; And the second is like unto it, you should love your neighbor as yourself. On these two commandments, all the law and order should be based.

Our problems began when some [of us— "popes and priests" described above] put themselves above the rest of us, or tried to.

They tried to convince us that *they* were more special and should be loved differently than the rest of us. To bring *their Self* more value and purpose, it was advantageous for them to change the first part of these two great commandments, so that the rest of us would love *them* more than we do our own *Selves*. They created a god who demanded to be worshipped, honored, and loved above anyone and all else. Then they claimed that God had chosen *them* as special siblings in our universal family unit, through whom God gave direction to the rest of us. This placed the control over society in *their* hands.

The human world in this solar system is progressively getting worse. It will continue to get worse until the two commandments above (about how a human should see their self and their neighbor) are properly implemented. These commandments must be applied to the laws that govern us. We must allow the power and control (through law and order) to maintain a consistent harmony of "one heart and one mind, where there are no poor among us."

Currently, there is no *moral compass* that is guiding humanity in the right direction.

There is no way we can be *full of pride* (prideful) if we love ourselves, and everyone else like we do ourselves. Self-love is part of our *ego*. Loving everyone else like we do ourselves depends on our opinion and beliefs about others. When humans divide themselves by borders, nations, languages, cultures, traditions, religions, and customs, *their pride* in these things will not allow them to love their neighbor as they do themselves.

Again, there is no advanced human society existing in the universe that is divided by borders, nations, languages, cultures, traditions, religions, or customs ... NOT A SINGLE ONE! None of the inhabitants of these worlds put themselves above others. None put others above themselves. In these advanced societies, the people are of one heart and one mind, and there is no money that exists, upon which one's personal possessions become more valued than another's.

No, these are not *communist* societies. There are many differing *personal* pursuits of happiness in these advanced worlds. Some of these pursuits require possessions in order to experience happiness. What is *equal* is that anyone who wants to have a pursuit of happiness that includes personal possessions, can obtain these possessions without money.

Only in underdeveloped human worlds will you find borders, nations, languages, cultures, traditions, religions, and customs. Again, in ALL advanced societies, none of these divisions or margins exist ... NOT A SINGLE ONE!

These things certainly exist in this world. They were meant to exist in this world. They are allowed in this world. The natural laws that support this solar system encourage and tolerate these divisions and societal margins. If this weren't the case, then the *measure of this earth's creation would not be fulfilled.*

Remember, people choose this underdeveloped conscious experience (life in this solar system) to test themselves and their humanity. At some point in their existence in the advanced worlds of our *Second Estate*, they became curious about this *feeling of deep pleasure or satisfaction derived from one's own achievements, the achievements of those with whom one is closely associated, or from qualities or possessions that are widely admired,* i.e., the feeling OF PRIDE.

Most everyone who chose to come to this earth, or who was forced to because of their behavior in an advanced society, wanted to be recognized for their own achievements. We didn't understand how having *pride* in our own accomplishments was such a bad thing for a human society. After the days of our probation living upon this earth, however, we will *finally* understand.

As we pointed out in a previous chapter, there are many people who come to this earth and ENJOY the feeling of pride. They ENJOY being recognized for their own accomplishments. They seek out and join groups of people with whom they become closely associated because they share similar feelings about their pride. They ENJOY having money and possessions and being widely admired for their worldly success. These people have learned something important about themselves: THEY LIKE PRIDE!

They like being separated into different family units and communities. They take a lot of pride in their own nations and the borders that protect their families and communities. They ENJOY believing that they are right and everyone else is wrong. They seek out religions that support the ENJOYMENT OF THEIR PRIDE. They find the god that is particular to them ... a god who chose just one family by which this god would bless the entire Earth. And THEY ENJOY THE FEELING of being a part of this family, either by birth or by adoption!

They ENJOY dressing according to *their group's* special garments (the clothes and accessories they wear that other people see and recognize as belonging to their particular group). They are not taught to love *themselves* with all of their heart, might, mind, and soul, but to love God instead. They ENJOY feeling that their leaders are special and have special assignments, given directly from God, to lead them and guide them. They ENJOY the moral compass that guides them to divide themselves from other, less worthy (according to their God's mandates) groups of people.

There's a popular song that makes most people *feel* a sense of connectedness with others. The song is called *Imagine*, by John Lennon. Regardless of the way the original lyrics were written, these groups could sing the song this way:

Imagine there's no heaven, except for ours.
It's easy if you try, because there's no hell for us,
That place is reserved for our neighbor, who isn't going to our heaven,
Above our group is only sky.
Imagine all the people, living for today, like we do.
Imagine there's no countries, except for ours.

It isn't hard to do. Those who kill or die for our country are heroes.

And there's no religion, too ... but ours.

Imagine all the people, living life in peace.

You may say I'm a dreamer, but I'm not the only one.

I hope someday you'll join our group, so the world can be one.

Imagine God coming again and calling forth our group as His only one.

When our God comes again, only our group will have the possessions.

I wonder if you can imagine this.

There won't be any greed or hunger, because we are God's brotherhood.

Imagine all the people, sharing all the world.

I hope someday you'll join us ... in our group ...

And the world will live as one, according to our group's imagination.

Is this how you would sing this song? How much *joy* do YOU get from belonging to a family unit, a community, and a nation? Are your race and culture special above others? Do you teach your children to carry *pride* in their hearts about their race, their heritage, their culture, their genealogy, their traditions, or their gender?

When you're in *your group* of people, among friends who dress like you, act like you, speak like you, and who ENJOY the same sense of PRIDE that you enjoy, are you happy? REALLY?

If you still want to kill yourself, then you must *not* be enjoying the feeling of *pride* too much. Do you find yourself alone and feeling dreary about finding a group of people to which you can connect and share in their PRIDE and JOY?

Is your life tedious, boring, dull ... dreary?

Perhaps you're not finding much joy living in a society of people who think more about *feeling prideful*, in all senses of the word, than they do about finding a way to connect to ALL OTHER PEOPLE with whom this group might not agree.

Perhaps you're still considering suicide because you're experiencing consciousness upon this earth, in this solar system, and still feel like this is a *lone and dreary world*.

LIFT UP YOUR HEAD AND REJOICE ...

The *pride thing* isn't working for you. You find *no joy* in any of the things that other people enjoy through their sense (feeling) of accomplishment in this world ... through their PRIDE.

You don't belong here. You're figuring this out for yourself.

You came. You saw. And you are very disappointed with the way things are going on this earth. You find NO ENJOYMENT here in this *lone and dreary world*.

You can leave, if YOU want.

But before you make that choice, consider some other cool things about the Real Truth® regarding our existence as advanced human beings going through a mortal conscious experience upon this earth.

Remember, YOU ARE GOD. THERE IS NO GOD BEFORE YOU, BEHIND YOU, OR AT YOUR SIDE.

Your future is in nobody's hands but YOURS.

The glory of God ... i.e., your advanced True Self, living in what we call our *Second Estate* ... is

INTELLIGENCE. Consider the knowledge of things as they *really* are, as we present it in the rest of this book. Keep in mind that *knowledge* is *not* INTELLIGENCE. *Intelligence* is the ability to act upon *knowledge*.

We've already explained to you why you chose to come to this earth. You're experiencing a lot of prideful people. From your own experience, which is the only proper way to gain *knowledge*, you are finding out what this attitude does to a society of human beings.

Once you have more *knowledge* about your *True Self*, you can then use your *intelligence ... that which makes you the most powerful life form that exists in your reality* ... to make the right choice about your continued existence upon this earth.

Whatever principle of intelligence we attain unto in this life, it will rise with us in the resurrection. And if a person gains more knowledge and intelligence in this life through [that person's] diligence and obedience than another, [this person] will have so much the advantage in the world to come.

"Diligence and obedience"? To what ... to whom?

TO YOUR TRUE SELF—THE GREATEST COMPENDIUM OF MATTER THAT EXISTS ANYWHERE IN THE UNIVERSE!

Chapter 7

Free Will

NOTHING is more important to human existence, where the purpose of this existence is for the individual to experience joy, than FREE WILL ... ABSOLUTELY NOTHING.

You have the free will to kill yourself if you want; and there's nothing that anybody, or any entity, in the universe can do to stop you. The exception, of course, is if you are tied down and constrained so that you *can't* kill yourself. It would follow, then, that your will (desire, determination, motivation, or resolve) to take your own life is not *always* based on *your* personal *free*dom to do so. Therefore, your will as a mortal is *not* always *free*, and cannot properly be called *free will*.

None of us *really* has free will here, because someone other than our own self can impede it. Couple this with the fact that our personal *freedom* and *will* are so important to our purpose for existing. How and why, then, can our individual mortal existence consequently be of any importance?

Again ... in spite of all the arguments about it ... NOTHING is more important to human existence, where the purpose of this existence is for the individual to experience joy, than FREE WILL ... ABSOLUTELY NOTHING.

What exactly is *free will?* And when was the last time you can remember using it in your personal pursuit of joy? Have you ever been *free* enough to do what you've wanted to do? Everyone seeks for their own personal pursuit of happiness. Has there ever been a time when you could follow the desires of *your* heart as an individual, regardless of being surrounded by so many others doing different things than you in their own pursuits of happiness?

The answer is YES. During your *First State of Conscious Existence*, your physical body was specifically and purposefully created to exercise unconditional and unabated FREE WILL. Where all other life forms were, are, and will always be created to do what their creators want them to do, ONLY HUMANS were created to do what the newly created individual wants to do themselves.

The main aspect that separates us from all other life forms is *free will* ... nothing more and nothing less. But in order to have this free will, we needed a physical body that would allow us to exercise it. This is why our bodies are similar to each other's, but completely distinct from all other life forms. We can see a group of any other life forms and immediately tell this group from all other groups. This is because all the members of other species look very, very similar. The human species is different. Our physical appearances (looks) are so individually unique that it is usually easy to tell us apart from the whole. We don't even need names to distinguish us from one another.

Our individual bodies can also influence our individual free will. In an advanced world, new people are not created with a gender. These advanced, newly created ones can choose their own gender whenever they want, or they can choose to remain ungendered. This is not the case in our current experience upon this earth.

Presently (2023), there is more argument about gender identity than many other issues. A person born into this world did *not* choose their own gender ... as far as their conscious free will is concerned ... in this, our *Third State of Conscious Existence*. Their gender was forced upon them. And when this forced gender starts to make them unhappy, they desire to change it.

Often, because of the restrictions and obstacles placed on their free will while living on this earth among others, the majority does not support gender transformations. Presently, a lot of hate and discord is experienced about these issues. Those who wish to change the identifying nature of their assigned gender at birth find it very difficult to do so. There is not much happiness in being told that you must accept the gender that was forced upon you at birth. Likewise, the fights and arguments that ensue regarding your ability to use free will to choose your own gender cause a lot of misery.

These gender issues join other contentious arguments, most of which revolve around free will. For another example, does a person whose physical body can create a new human (the majority views these humans as female mothers) have the right to end the development of the new body going on inside her womb?

There are many other sources of human contention as well. This contention, however, cannot always be blamed on the ignorant majority. Some people vociferously (vocally, loudly) ... in their PRIDE (ah ... there's that word again) confront and intimidate others. Shouldn't the majority have the free will to walk on a public sidewalk or drive to the store without this intimidation? They too want *their* free will to be supported and protected.

Fights ensue, divisions are made, and PRIDE—on both sides of the issues—continues to do what it has always done: destroy human peace and happiness. In a world full of PRIDE, is it possible for everyone living on the planet to have and exercise *free will?* No, it is not possible. Where there is PRIDE ... as it has been systematically and persistently reiterated throughout this book ... there can be no peace. There can be no true justice.

Consider the signs held up during the protests of people wanting to assert *their free will* over others': "NO JUSTICE. NO PEACE." The protestors exercise their free will to break laws, intimidate others, and be loud and obnoxious. These are not allowing others to exercise the option that *they* should be afforded in exercising *their* free will.

Then there are laws that codify (incorporate) moral codes established by one group trying to support and protect *their free will* by taking away the same from others: "You obey *our laws* or we will take away your freedom." Which laws are the *right* laws? In two of the previous chapters, we explained the only way that *righteousness* (the right way) can be achieved. It is the only way to unite humanity and stop people from killing each other. What we wrote includes words taken from a story taught by one of the world's main religions. We wrote:

Humanity will never survive unless the societies that sustain our existence establish law and order based on the following two important principles about human existence—who we are:

First, love yourself with all your heart, and with all your soul, and with all your mind; And the second is like unto it, you should love your neighbor as yourself. On these two commandments, all the law and order should be based.

This particular religious deity (god), upon whose legend and teachings the above story was taken, also taught people not to argue with each other and call each other "fools." He taught that we should not sue each other in court; and if we're sued, we should not fight back. In fact, he taught us to turn the other cheek and to never fight back. In one of his finest counsels, he encapsulated this simple rule of a *righteous* law ... as it should be:

Love your enemies, bless them that curse you, do good to them that hate you, and pray for them which despitefully use you, and persecute you.

Nobody in this world does this, especially not those whose hearts and minds are full of PRIDE.

So, when was it, as it pertains to your existence on this earth, in this solar system, that you exercised unconditional free will? It would be better asked, "Was there ever a time in your existence on the earth when you *started* to exercise your free will, before someone else started obstructing and hindering it? Was there ever a time when YOU acted independently of any prior event or state of the universe?"

Yes, you did, when you were a little child. Because you couldn't remember any event before you became conscious in this *earth experience*, as a little child you acted independently of any prior event. But, as we have explained, there was actually a *state of consciousness* (in the universe) that *foundationalized* your ability to exercise free will. It was during this *First State of existence in the First Estate* that you became a human—not a dog or a cat—a human with unconditional free will.

Before we discuss more about the nature and purpose of human free will, it would perhaps be beneficial to your curiosity and intelligence to explore what people in our world think about free will. As with *everything*, there are all kinds of arguments about what *free will* means. Generally, science and philosophy define it as:

> The supposed power or capacity of humans to make decisions or perform actions independently of any prior event or state of the universe. Arguments for free will have been based on the subjective experience of freedom, on sentiments of guilt, on revealed religion, and on the common assumption of individual moral responsibility that underlies the concepts of law, reward, punishment, and incentive. (See "free will," Britannica.com, 2023.)

Then there's religion. Religion establishes

> sentiments of guilt ... on the common assumption of individual moral responsibility that underlies the concepts of law, reward, punishment, and incentive. In theology, the existence of free will must be reconciled with God's omniscience [infinite knowledge] and benevolence [kindness] and with divine grace, which allegedly is necessary for any meritorious act [whether a person gets to go to heaven or not].

If there is a God, and this god created us for Himself by his own goodwill and nature (grace), then we cannot have *true* individual free will. We must act according to God's commandments and *His will*. If we don't, we do not merit His grace and blessings. This is not Real Truth®. This is not how things were, are, or will be.

Our human existence cannot and should not be based on *any god's* will. It should be based upon OUR OWN FREE WILL. Again and again ... in spite of all the arguments about it ... NOTHING is more important to human existence, where the purpose of this existence is for the individual to experience joy, than FREE WILL ... ABSOLUTELY NOTHING.

But what if there really was a god who was omniscient, omnipotent, and omnipresent (all-knowing, all-powerful, and present everywhere throughout the universe)? What if this god came down to the earth as a mortal human in order to show us an example of what kind of people we should be?

This would make a lot of sense. If not even God—as a mortal living upon this earth—can keep His own commandments, then how can we? This compassionate and wise god should come and live among us and, at least, teach us what we need to do to save ourselves from each other.

Above, we quoted from traditional stories presented by one of the most popular religious belief systems in the world. The scripture this church touts as the "keystone" of its religion teaches that God *did* come down in the flesh, as His own Son, to give us His commandments and save us from ourselves. One of this particular religion's sects presents in their own scriptures how well God was received by the people living upon Earth:

> God himself shall come down among the children of men, and shall redeem his people. And because he dwelleth in flesh he shall be called the Son of God, and having subjected the flesh to the will of the Father, being the Father and the Son—The Father, because he was conceived by the power of God; and the Son, because of the flesh; thus becoming the Father and Son—And they are one God, yea, the very Eternal Father of heaven and of earth. And thus the flesh becoming subject to the Spirit, or the Son to the Father, being one God, suffereth temptation, and yieldeth not to the temptation, but suffereth himself to be mocked, and scourged, and cast out, and disowned by his people.

It should be noted here once more, that this particular sect has a disproportionate number of its members committing suicide and taking antidepressants. Additionally, this sect has become the wealthiest church on Earth! These two facts, when analyzed properly, according to the effect they have on the members, reveal the true cause of all of this emotional depression.

Why are these people committing suicide and taking so many drugs? This church tells its members to follow the example of Jesus and obey the commandments that he gave as the "Son of God" when he lived upon the earth. But then, these members compare the teachings of their God ("Heavenly Father") and Jesus Christ to their leaders' teachings, especially about what people need to do to be "redeemed." Incredibly, the saving focus is *not* established and based on loving yourself and your neighbor as yourself, but on having PRIDE that you belong to "God's only true church," which is led by "God's only true appointed leaders."

As in *all* religious sects, of *all* religions that claim to have "God's only truth," the *free will* of the people in this church is profoundly affected and controlled. Members are taught to heed God's will, but *only* as it is "revealed through His servants"—the accepted "prophets, seers, and revelators." Further, they are instructed to obey these leaders, even if they contradict their own scriptures (which they do).

When each person is born into this world, their free will is largely unconditional and unimpeded. The little child is curious about their new world. They explore and find many new things. They see new things, they hear new things, they smell new things, and they even put these new things into their mouths to be tasted. But the moment the child acts in a way that is not how the parent *believes* the child should act, guilt is introduced.

This guilt is the underlying cause of the rewards, punishments, and incentives that will be the basis of what the child does and why the child does what they do. The child's free will is greatly impeded by their parent's free will. If the child complies with the will of the parent, then the child is rewarded. If not, the child is punished. There is no incentive for the child to exercise their own free will ... not in this world.

As we have explained, there is an energy that we call the *eternal soul*, which connects to a newly created infant's body when it takes its first breath. This unique form of energy identifies the individual from the rest of the human "forms of energy" that exist throughout the universe. This "soul" was *foundationalized* a long time ago, in a solar system, in a galaxy, that could be trillions of light years away from this earth.

We have explained what human experience and consciousness are, according to Real Truth®. We have explained that this *form of energy* is established and stored on the *Intergalactic Internet Cloud* ... for want of a better way to describe it ... that is responsible for giving consciousness to all living things. We've explained how we did not exist until some other human being created a *human brain*, so that this unique physical part of a body could connect *to the Cloud* in order to upload and download information.

The first information we gained about our personal and individual identity were the experiences that we had while living with our Creator in their solar system. As we had these experiences, they were all uploaded and stored on *the Cloud* in a specific file, to which only each of us, as individuals, have the *proper password*. No one else can access our information—not even our Creators. No matter where we might go in the universe, we can access our *individual information* ... the energy that is personal to our unique existence.

We were *not* created to be someone else's servant. We were *not* created and foundationalized to be under the control of any other person or entity, god or not. WE WERE CREATED TO *BE* GODS—THE GREATEST LIFE FORM POSSIBLE.

In essence, because our personal information (experience) is stored on the *Intergalactic Cloud*, we ARE *omnipresent* (present everywhere throughout the universe). We ARE also *omniscient* (all-knowing) in regard to our own information, which can only be accessed for our own will and pleasure. We ARE also *omnipotent* (all-powerful), because no one can control what we do or how we do it. We are the ONLY god that matters in our existence.

No one is allowed to create new human beings properly, unless they have been commissioned and can be trusted to do it correctly. Unlike our Earth parents, our *true advanced parent* created us in *their own image*, not gendered unless we, through our own experience, wanted to be. We were created by gods to become gods. And until we became an omniscient, omnipresent, and omnipotent life form

... a god ... we remained with the advanced humans who gave us life. They oversaw our development and made sure that *our free will* took precedence over *theirs*.

These advanced creators did not teach us to worship and serve God. They created us to become our own God!

You do not tell a god what to do or how to do it. But if you can convince a person that they are *not* a god, and that there exists a god whom the person should be serving and worshipping, then the person loses *their* free will to the will of whomever is deceiving the person about a more powerful entity than their own *TRUE SELF*.

In our *First Estate*, we learned that the kingdom of God is *truly within*, and there is only one KING or QUEEN sitting upon the throne therein.

As we had experience, in the form of energy, this energy was stored *on the Cloud under our unique identifying classification*. This *eternal file* established a *data set* that was full of everything that we wanted to store there. When we graduated and became our own God, we relied on this *eternal data* as the basis for our unique, individual existence ... no matter where this existence might take place throughout the endless and eternal universe. In order to have these new experiences in other worlds, worlds without end, we needed a body that had a brain. This would be the appropriate hardware and software that would allow us to access and download all of our previously stored personal experiences. These experiences made us who we are as unique individuals.

The information that was *foundationalized* in our *data set stored on the eternal Intergalactic Cloud* was sometimes hard to download into the new body. When we couldn't download what was stored in our unique files, we felt a physical feeling of frustration that we now call *unhappiness*. Most of the time, the *processor* (our brain) wasn't the right one to accomplish the job of downloading or uploading our individual information properly.

It was our mission and desire, as we traveled throughout the universe, or rather, allowed our personal data to exist connected to the universal *Cloud*, to find the *right physical brain with the right processor*. Only with the right processor can we find and experience what we can now describe as "joy." If the processor is flawed in some way, it isn't going to do what we expect it to do. With the right processor, we can upload and download our unique information into the brain of the new physical body ... according to OUR FREE WILL.

No person or entity ... and there's no entity greater than the human life form ... can access our information and download it into their own experience, UNLESS we give them permission to do so. This is how relationships with other humans are established. We share some of the information from our *stored files* with some of the information from *their stored files* to create a *new file*. As long as this *new file* ... this new experience ... is not corrupted, we will enjoy accessing it, along with the person with whom we have shared our experiences (in a new sub-file stored on the *eternal Intergalactic Cloud-based hard drive*).

If anyone attempts to force us to create a *new file* with them, without our consent, or to serve *their desires* that have nothing to do with our own, the file becomes corrupted, and our brain senses the discomfort.

For the reasons given above, many people want to disconnect *their file* from the corrupt one. When a person commits suicide, the person immediately disconnects the *eternal energy of their soul* from the relationships (new files) established in the world in which these *new files* were created.

Again, and again, and again ...

NOTHING is more important to human existence—where the purpose of this existence is for the individual to experience joy—than FREE WILL ... ABSOLUTELY NOTHING.

Chapter 8

The End of the World

A world ended on October 13, 2019. On this day, the planet Fortnite, along with all of its inhabitants, was destroyed.

The millions of humans interacting and participating with each other on planet Fortnite—each doing their own thing, in their own way—saw an incredible explosion. Then, everything (including their avatars) was sucked into a big black hole. There had been an environment of land, water, plants, and animals, where these humans interacted with each other on a daily basis. After the explosion, only a black hole remained in a virtual universe that very few of the human players understood.

The humans were emotionally "blown away" at the thought that the world in which they had spent many hours playing during their life, no longer existed. How could these humans be emotionally affected by the destruction of this world, unless they were still alive and conscious of the fact that their planet Fortnite had been destroyed by the creation of a black hole?

Obviously, these humans weren't actually living on planet Fortnite. Each had chosen a personal avatar to live on the planet and participate with other Fortnite avatars. Their real Self actually existed outside of Fortnite's virtual universe in another, parallel one.

While people were having experiences on Fortnite (seeing and hearing things) through their chosen avatars, their actual, physical body was present in another world—in their real Earth world. But while their minds (at least their eyes and ears) were experiencing life on planet Fortnite, there seemed to be no other planet. Their eyes and ears were so focused on what their avatars were experiencing (seeing and hearing), that they became oblivious to what was happening around them in their real world.

All of a sudden, with warning only of an impending "event," the people saw and heard an explosion, and then nothing but darkness surrounding a black hole. Their Fortnite life experience was over. Their avatars were all dead. But their real Selves were still alive. Millions of people, just like themselves, experienced the death of their own avatar. Now, no one was able to connect to planet Fortnite and experience life there any longer.

People were disappointed, at least the ones who were having a good life and winning at the Fortnite experience. The others who were not winning—those who were always getting killed on planet Fortnite—weren't as bothered by the abrupt way the game ended.

There were millions of other people who wanted to play on Fortnite. Many of these were watching what was going on. These observers realized that if they actually joined in, they would soon be killed by those who knew how to play the game better than they did. To these millions of observers, and the millions of others who were quickly and easily overpowered and killed by the more experienced ones, the game wasn't fair. It wasn't worth playing.

Fortnite is just a game. What is described above is exactly what happened on October 13, 2019. Just two days later, the game's creators released "Chapter 2," and life on planet Fortnite began again. This time, though, the playing field was a bit more equal and fair. This time, so hoped the creators, more people would join in and play the game. The creators released a statement about the new improvements they had made, saying, "More Fun, Less Grind."

Consider the type of computer games that will be played in the future. At the time of this writing, technology is advancing faster than at any other time in human history. Game engineers are working quickly and successfully at finding a way to create a pathway between a game player's brain and the computer's software. Instead of just seeing and hearing what happens in a game, players will soon be able to use their other senses to smell, taste, and feel things found in the game's environment.

Science is exploring the human brain and beginning to understand how the brain can create a very real dream experience. This understanding will eventually lead to the invention of interfaces between computer software and a person's brain that can create an artificial dream inside of a person's mind, a virtual reality that is just as real as their own dreams. With this advanced technology, perhaps each game might come with a warning:

CAUTION: Real sensory experience is part of the interactive platform of this game. You will see, hear, smell, taste, and feel things in the game's environment that seem real. No part of this game will cause any real, physical damage to your body, or end your life. But all interactions will be felt through your sensory receptors as if they were real. For example, if you get shot by a gun, you will feel the bullet. If you get sliced by a sword, you will feel the cut.

Advanced technology will allow one's "real" reality to be altered for the time that the person is playing the game. As the player's brain interacts within the game, the experience will seem just as real as their life experience is when they are not playing the game; or just as real as their dreams seem to be as they are experienced in the subconscious mind. Based on the reality of what is happening with the advancements made in gaming, consider what computer games might be like on Earth hundreds of thousands of years into the future.

Some young Fortnite players were asked how they felt after the game ended in an explosion and they were left without the ability to play the game for a couple of days. Their general response reflected the reason why they started playing the game in the first place: they were bored.

If humans on planet Earth learn how to live together in peace and harmony, where there is no want or need, then humanity could continue into the future, indefinitely. In this perfect human world, each person could experience life according to each of their individual desires of happiness, based on the principles of unconditional free will. However, after living in a perfect world for a while, one could become bored. We would want to play games in order to entertain ourselves and gain new experiences that we otherwise could not have in our unchanging and unchallenging perfect world.

In the world of Fortnite, boredom doesn't exist. Players try to stay alive while everyone else in the world is trying their best to eliminate them. A game that starts out with 100 players will end with only one. The players seek for weapons and resources in order to achieve Victory Royale (in other words, to be the last player standing in each game).

Players may participate in as many as 10–30 (or more) games in a day, each time with an avatar of their choosing. V-bucks are used to purchase items that create value and individuality, which is an important aspect of the game. The more V-bucks a player has, the more fun it is because there are more options for creativity while playing the game.

The creators of Fortnite observed the inequality of the players' skill levels. They wanted to make the game fairer ("More Fun, Less Grind") to attract other players, especially the millions who were just watching. To change the game, the same people who created the world destroyed it and set up a new one.

Fortnite's creators are actually Fortnite's gods. They created the virtual experience for a specific purpose. They ended it for a specific purpose. We would like to think they ended their Fortnite world for a good purpose for all players—to bring more equality, more fairness, and more fun. But chances are high that they ended one virtual world—from which they were making a lot of money—in order to create another one … from which they would make even more.

The new players who take part in the game know very little about how the world was created or how to properly play the game long enough without being killed too soon. As a new person starts to play, their inexperience makes them vulnerable to the more experienced players who have the most weapons and resources and, therefore, the most power.

Let's pretend that Fortnite is the only game in town; that it is the best game to play in order to play with the most people and have the best gaming experience. Let's suppose that there is no other gaming platform (no other virtual world) available where a person can join others and spend time interacting to relieve boredom.

Let's say that there are 15 billion people who want to play the game. Most of them are just observers. These remain 'observers only' because they realize that they could never win, so why start to play? They realize that they wouldn't be given a fair chance to live for more than just a few minutes before being killed. This is because of the power and experience from within the game of the few who control it.

Those who created the game are much more powerful than those who control the game from within. However, none of the creators (outside of the game) could do much within the game, if they were to join in and start playing. As players themselves, the creators wouldn't have any more advantage within the game than any of the other players. But outside of the game, as the game's creators, they can destroy the world and create a new one that would attract more players.

The creators know that there are millions of people sitting on the sidelines just observing. Those who are just watching are potential customers. If they chose to play, these people would further fulfill the purpose for which the world was created for the Fortnite creators: to make money.

But what if the game was actually created by the 15 billion people as a place where they could interact with each other so that they weren't bored with their regular life? What if the game was the only game in town, the only way that the 15 billion people could have some fun interacting with each other in a virtual world (the opposite of being bored)?

If the purpose of the game was to engage as many people as possible in the experience, finding a way to make it enjoyable for those just watching would be important. But what if just a few players were spoiling it for the rest? Why wouldn't the 15 billion people want to destroy what they created and start over again?

The Real Truth® is ... mortal life upon planet Earth is nothing more or less than a very sophisticated and highly advanced human interactive world. This world is being experienced by each mortal's higher, advanced True Self. We are actually a highly advanced human race living in another, parallel universe.

There are approximately 15 billion of us living on different planets in a mutually shared solar system. We live in the perfect world for us, which we created for us, according to each of our individual desires of happiness. The mortal experience on planet Earth is the only way that we can interact with each other while living on these different, advanced planets.

Think of it this way:

Let's suppose that all nine planets of our current solar system were inhabited by humans. The planets were created to be new homes for people who once lived together on the same planet called Earth. Advanced science allowed us to create these new planets so that we could spread our population throughout the solar system. Let's suppose that these new planets were highly advanced and provided a perfect life for each inhabitant.

While living on these perfect worlds, we would get bored. We've conquered death and disease. We do not allow plants and animals (nor bacteria nor viruses) that might threaten human life, to exist on our new planets. Living for a long time among the same people, we learn everything that there is to know about the people sharing our planet. But we don't know much about the people who are living on the other planets.

So that we don't get bored with the same people on our perfect planet, we desire to become involved with those living on the other planets in our solar system. To involve ourselves with these others, and not have to travel to their planet (which is their home, not ours), we connect to an Intergalactic Internet platform. (If we visited their home planet, it might disrupt the balance of their society, just as their visiting our planet might disrupt the balance of our perfect society.)

This vast Internet platform would be powered by our solar system's sun. We would all have mutual access to this virtual world, to which we could connect equally at the speed of light. Earth would be our Fortnite. The platform in which Earth exists would be the universe that we currently observed from Earth. (However, to our True Self, our real universe is not Earth's universe. To us, as advanced humans, Earth exists in a virtual or parallel universe.)

We start interacting with each other by playing the game of mortal life on Earth. At first, it all goes pretty well. It starts out equal for all, with plenty of room and resources for everyone. Because the game platform allows free will, the players can create whatever kind of world they want, as long as they are able to convince the other players (or force them) to accept it. Some of the other players learn how to control the game and take it over. Soon, the world becomes corrupted by these few, who eventually take over the world.

Now the *earth experience* that started out equal for all becomes one where people are dependent on others for their survival. No advanced human can connect to the corrupted game and remain alive without another, more experienced player helping them learn how to play. A player can't just connect to the *earth experience* with a game avatar of their own creation, one that looks like them as an advanced adult. The game has changed drastically from what it was in the beginning.

Now, in order to connect to the game, an advanced human has to wait until a mortal body has developed inside the womb of one of the other players. They have to be "born" into the world before they can start playing. Once the new body is fully formed and functional, the first breath an infant takes becomes the connective protocol of (way to participate in) the mortal experience upon Earth. (Some call this the "breath of life.")

This mortal experience is nothing like it was meant to be, as Earth's creators intended for it to be, in the beginning. Earth's creators do not want it to end. But if the players inside the game do not do something to improve the playing field and return it to how it used to be in the beginning, the world will not fulfill the *measure* of its creation. If Earth does not provide the experience it was meant to provide for those who want to play the game, then it will be destroyed by the "gods" (advanced humans) who created it.

WE (each and every one of us—YOU included) created Earth. WE are these gods. Earth will be destroyed by US—the advanced human beings who want to play the game of mortal life.

Life upon Earth has been going on for billions of years. During those years, our True Selves (who we really are) have tried everything that can possibly be done to convince our mortal avatars to start playing the game as it was meant to be played. This was all done according to the laws of nature (the rules of the game). We have failed.

Now the rules must be bent as a last resort.

Our mortal avatars were not supposed to know and understand that they are not the real person behind their existence. Because if mortals actually knew this, then any time they experienced an uncomfortable situation that made them unhappy, they would end their own existence.

158

You will know this Real Truth® when you die. When your mortal life ends, no matter how it ends, you will immediately be aware that you continue to exist. You will recognize that your True Self is an advanced human of incredible intelligence and individual power (free will). You will then know that YOU are the only god that has ever existed in your experience.

You will realize that all the times upon Earth when you felt the presence of "God" or your "conscience," you were actually feeling the connection that your mortal avatar had with your True Self. You will not only know these Real Truth®s about your own Self, but also about every other human with whom you shared your earthly experience. You will know that each person who lives on Earth is actually connected to their True Self. You will know that there is no other god outside of YOU, outside of EACH of US.

At that time, you will recognize exactly what has corrupted the mortal experience and destroyed humanity. You will understand that, unless confronted and eliminated, this culprit (this CAUSE of the problem), will destroy our Fortnite—end our lives upon Earth.

This culprit is PRIDE.

PRIDE lies to us and tells us that we are not our own god, but are subjected to (or enslaved by) others who control our actions. PRIDE teaches us to not depend on ourselves for our own salvation. PRIDE teaches us that we must depend on our own achievements, the achievements of those with whom we are closely associated, or on qualities or possessions that are widely admired by others.

We are taught to embrace PRIDE as a "righteous" attribute by those who personally benefit from the lie. If we could be convinced of two things, we might be able to unite and do what must be done in order to save Earth and all of humanity. First, we must understand that there is no controlling power above US—outside of the god who sits upon a throne in the Kingdom of God *Within*. Second, we must recognize that WE are responsible for our own salvation and happiness. Thus convinced, PRIDE would no longer exist, and those who promoted it for their own gain might cry out, "Oh mountains and rocks, fall on us, and hide us from this Real Truth®!"

But PRIDE does exist and is destroying humanity. PRIDE will eventually lead to our *True Selves* recognizing and accepting the futility of this solar system's existence. Thus convinced, we will end it, so that we can start a new one somewhere else in our galaxy, one that can *fulfill the measure of our creation*—in the pursuit of our individual happiness.

Chapter 9

The Futility of Nothingness

Science has a theory that, in the beginning, before anything existed—nothing existed; and in the end, nothing will exist again. If science is correct, what would be the point or usefulness of being a human? Our existence would be one of *futility*.

Has the information presented in this book helped you decide *to be, or not to be*? Has it convinced you to continue to live? Or has it persuaded you to go ahead and end your existence? Will you be able to tell everyone else in your world to listen to and consider the information? Perhaps you will be able to honestly and courageously exclaim this:

> These are true messengers. I exhort you to give strict heed to their counsel and teachings, and they will lead you in the way of life and salvation.

Or does this information confront your PRIDE, causing a feeling of enmity (discomfort) in your cognitive paradigms (thinking patterns), and causing your PRIDE to respond like this:

> Ah! You have looked over my kingdom and my greatness and glory. Now you want to take possession of the whole of it.

The overall message of this information is that YOU are the greatest! It teaches you that YOU already have the power within you to save yourself and change your life. "Yeah, but many, many other *new age* philosophies teach that as well," you might say.

There are many (too many) self-help gurus who say all kinds of things to empower you to take control of your life. But how is their information (or even ours) relevant to a teenage girl forced into prostitution because her family doesn't have enough money to provide the basic necessities of life? This information means ABSOLUTELY NOTHING and is certainly not relevant to the daily struggles of people existing each day on this earth.

How can we convince you that FREE WILL is the most important part of being a human when you don't seem to have it? You're forced to get out of bed each day and struggle to provide yourself and your loved ones with the basic necessities that are required to exist. You're FORCED to work for someone who will pay you the money you need to survive.

How can we convince you that your life is worth living, when your parents created you—more likely than not, by accident—because their hormones affected their free will?

Most children are provided with the ability to pursue their own desires of happiness for a few years. After this brief freedom, how is it a wonderful thing to be alive when you are *forced* to give up your childlike pursuit of happiness and, instead, work by the sweat of your brow? If you don't, you will die from starvation, thirst, inadequate housing, insufficient healthcare, and very little opportunity for learning.

162

How is it a wonderful life when most people living on the earth never reach old age and, instead, die of natural causes? Most people commit suicide ... involuntarily, because they can't afford nutritious food and proper housing. The majority of the leading causes of death in the United States revolve around an improper diet. (Suicide ranks as the 11th leading cause.) Because nobody forces you to put things in your mouth, then you are committing suicide involuntarily by what you eat. But you're still the one causing your own death.

What about dangerous work conditions? What about the continual bloodshed from war and terrible governments, most of which are put into power by your FREE WILL, through democracy?

What about the fact that as soon as you are born ... the very day of the beginning of your life ... your body starts to die? Most physical bodies, regardless of how healthy they are, will only last several decades living on this earth. Why would you want to continue living on this earth with the type of body that was passed on to you through imperfect and corrupt DNA? How many of the diseases that can end your life early, are inherited?

What good is it going to do you if all of the information we have provided throughout this book is the Real Truth®—things as they *really* are? Upon knowing how things *really* are after death (in a post-mortal existence), why would you spend even one more day suffering the misery that you are experiencing in life on this earth?

We know that what we have presented to you is things as they *really* are. But what good is it going to do you, if you believe us? If it were possible to catch a glimpse of what our conscious existence is going to be like after we die, we would be stupid for not ending our *earth experience* NOW!

We (the authors of this book) are certainly not fools, and we have no PRIDE in ourselves. Like you, we have an *ego* that gives us our self-esteem and personal value, but we experience no "feeling of deep pleasure or satisfaction derived from one's own achievements, the achievements of those with whom one is closely associated, or from qualities or possessions that are widely admired." If writing this book was about PRIDE, we would have revealed our true identities and charged money for this information.

We also do not have any delusional or grandiose expectations about the effect that this book will have on this world. As we explained in a previous chapter, even if there were a God, and God came down and tried to teach the Real Truth® to people upon this earth, God would be rejected, spit upon, and killed. We know that very few, if any, will accept the information about who we are as humans and why we exist. Personal PRIDE is too powerful. The achievements you make in your life (PRIDE) are too important to your existence.

Furthermore, we did *not* present all the information that we know about planet Earth, this solar system, and the five different times during this planet's existence when humanity rose to great heights of innovation, technology, and achievement. These experiences only caused humans to become more divided, eventually leading to the demise of the human race (for the most part).

164

It won't do us any good to explain that, when humans are cooperating and taking control and dominion over the earth, the earth naturally warms because of human activity. When this *warming activity* ceases—or is greatly diminished because most humans have been destroyed—an *ice age* develops on the earth. (Go ahead! Google how many different times there has been an *ice age* on this earth ... according to scientific opinion.)

We know that, because humanity has failed five times in the past, there is not much hope in believing that this time around ... during this *Sixth Dispensation of Time* ... humans will get it right. We DO know the following, based on our research and the ancient records available to us: There has never been another time during the history of this solar system when the Real Truth® about who we are and why we exist has been completely revealed. (Unfortunately, the PRIDE of science cannot accept this fact without diminishing its own importance and achievements.)

Humans who are going through this *earth experience* are NOT supposed to have this information. There is a good reason for this. If they had it, most of them would commit suicide. Then they would return to being the incredible, advanced humans that we all are ... that you will consciously recognize yourself as, after your mortal brain stops working.

Humanity has failed to get it right during five different time periods of Earth's existence, when none of the Real Truth® about human existence was available. We knew this and persuaded ourselves to have enough *faith* in order to have *hope* (inspired by our egos, not our pride). We hoped that if we gave people living on the earth one more chance, they just might make things right and save humanity. In saving humanity, they would save the solar system in which humans are given the opportunity to exist differently than they do as their advanced, eternal selves.

You don't need to believe us. Few do. There were true messengers living on the earth in the not-too-distant past who also tried to help people. These were rejected and killed. For this reason, we remain anonymous and hide our whereabouts. Additionally, so that this information can be available and accessible to anyone, especially to the poor who can barely afford to provide for themselves, we do not charge for it.

Let's briefly review this information before we end our attempt to share what we know:

The energy that fuels the consciousness of *any* life form that exists in the universe is what appears as the darkness of space. (Science likes to call this *dark matter.*) There is no space or place where *nothing* exists. The basic elements that make up all *matter* constitute the *energy* that is responsible for each *thing*, living or non-living.

Nothing can appear, or be created, without *something* acting upon it. As science develops a keener and clearer understanding of how *dark matter* works, humans will create new moons and planets for this solar system. The *energy* that creates the elementary basis of all things, is the same for humans as it is for all other *things* found throughout

166

the universe. The only difference is the physical nature of the body that houses the central nuclear reactor (the brain) responsible for a living *thing's* ability to act and be acted upon in any environment. The human brain is much different than any other life form's brain ... MUCH DIFFERENT.

It takes a human to create a human. A dog cannot create a human, but a human can create a dog. If a new human is created involuntarily—by the force of sexual-hormonal-based desire—this type of body will not, and cannot, be an unconditionally FREE-WILLED life form. If a newly created human being is going to have *free will*, they must be provided with the proper body and environment in which free will can exist. Our current solar system does *not* allow for unconditional free will. All things that are part of *our* current solar system were made to serve the needs and wants of particular earthly creators.

It takes a very special person to be the *proper* human creator. NONE of these types of people exist in this solar system. In other solar systems, in other galaxies, in other parts of the universe, these special human creators live. They create new human bodies that allow the new life form to act and be acted upon by free will, thus creating a unique individual that can ONLY be human, like the creator. We have called this *state of existence* our *First Estate*.

After existing for a long period of time, during which time we used our free will to explore the universe and all it has to offer, we eventually determined what kind of life experience we wanted for ourselves—an experience that corresponded with how we developed as an individual in our *First Estate*.

Once we determined what kind of advanced human being we wanted to be, we looked for a place where other humans who shared our same *humanity type*, or rather, our same desires for happiness, already lived.

When we found this solar system, we asked a person living there to create a body for us, so that we could connect to the experience and participate in this new solar system. Once the body was created according to our unique specifications, we connected the *energy of our eternal soul* to this new body in our new *eternal home*. Once properly connected, there was no longer any need for us to stay in our Creator's solar system. We left home to establish our own life. We voluntarily chose to end our existence (i.e., committed suicide) in order to be able to live our new life. Thus ended our existence in our *First Estate* and began our *Second Estate*.

Our new world became our *Second Estate*. In this *state of consciousness*, our *eternal soul* remains connected to the physical body that was prepared for us on that planet. This allows us to live in our new home for as long as we desire.

We began to share experiences with others. Our new experiences soon replaced our first experiences that we gained as newly created people living in our *First Estate*. Our new relationships in the *Second Estate* filled the longing and desire we developed by being created in a societal structure, similar to all other human societies found throughout the universe. We see as we are seen, and know as we are known.

In associating with others, a few of us were not satisfied with just our egos—our sense of self-importance and value. These few longed for more experiences that could not be lived in the solar system that we call our *eternal home*. PRIDE (as it has been repetitively defined throughout this book) began to tempt us.

We had already established a personal relationship with others who supported our mutual egos. So when a few of us gave in to this temptation of PRIDE, the others had to decide whether to follow along into a *Third Estate* or remain behind. Knowing the consequences that we would have to endure by "partaking of the Tree" of our *Third Estate*, most of us were reluctant to "eat this fruit."

The consequences of living in the solar system in which planet Earth is found were properly and clearly explained to us. We were warned. But we knew that we had free will to choose for ourselves. Most people chose *not to partake* and instead remained in the *Second Estate*, hoping that the person who was valued by their ego learned that it was probably not the right choice to want to live on this earth (the *Third Estate*). Nevertheless, there were a few who followed their desires to not be alone and lose the valued relationship: "Then I will partake."

None of us had to partake of this particular *tree*. We lived in a kind of *Garden of Eden*, in which there were all kinds of "Trees of Life" from which we could eat abundantly. This means we could choose from a wide variety of solar systems available in our *Second Estate*. (For want of a better way to explain it, our *Milky Way Galaxy* is this *Second Estate—our Garden of Eden*. The billions of solar systems in this galaxy are the "trees of life" from which we can freely eat. But we were warned *not* to go to this particular solar system, where the earth we are currently on exists, and "partake" of life here. Again, it was not necessary to our happiness.)

Those who wanted to go to Earth to experience life there, regardless of the consequences (which they knew about in advance), were LIED TO AND DECEIVED BY THEIR PRIDE. They convinced themselves that living on the earth would give them a better "feeling of deep pleasure or satisfaction derived from one's own achievements, the achievements of those with whom one is closely associated, or from qualities or possessions that are widely admired."

And thus, their PRIDE became the "father of lies."

At first, the bodies created for the *earth experience* were *not* created through the sexual process. By and by, sex was the only process that was used to create new bodies for the *earth experience*. (This is part of the information that we are withholding for now.)

As an earth-bound mortal, you cannot remember that you are actually a highly advanced human participating in a *dream-like* experience. Your only reality is living in what you now experience as a "lone and dreary world." You are not *consciously* connected to your *True Self* still existing in your *Second Estate*.

While on Earth, not having any knowledge of who you *really* are and why you *really* exist, you seek for knowledge. Not being able to figure things out for yourself, you ask other people living on the earth, if they know. A few people, controlled by the "father of lies," by their PRIDE, answer your sincere prayers to know, with: "I hear you. What is it that you want?" While leaders *do* play some role in this, you don't recognize that it is *your own* PRIDE that hears and answers your prayers.

Not having any direct access to your *True Self*, you are misled and given all kinds of misinformation that becomes a mass of confusion to you. To help you to learn the answers to the questions about your own reality, that your mortal brain does not allow you to remember or understand, you seek for "messengers."

Luckily, there are a few people living on Earth with you who are unaffected by PRIDE. These have no "feeling of deep pleasure or satisfaction derived from one's own achievements, the achievements of those with whom one is closely associated, or from qualities or possessions that are widely admired."

We are these people. We are True Messengers. Our minds are not clouded with PRIDE. Somehow, for the sake of everyone, we are able to be directly connected to our *True Self*, living in our *Second Estate*. Being thus connected, we can tell you who you *really* are and why you *really* exist. If you give strict heed to our counsel and teachings, we can lead you in the way of life and salvation.

But how can you believe us? How do you know that we are True Messengers who know the Real Truth® about all things? You can try and test us. You can ask us questions about things that you are not allowed to remember (that are not revealed to your mortal, Earth-based mind). If what we tell you makes sense and disperses the cloud of confusion in your mind, then, and only then, will you know that we are True Messengers.

However, it really doesn't matter if you listen to or believe us, or not. You can buy anything in this world for money. A person can find a self-help guru and pay for whatever information supports their PRIDE.

You can know everything that a True Messenger knows, simply by committing suicide and returning to your *Second Estate*, where you live as the greatest life form that exists in your reality. You will realize that you existed before connecting your *soul* to the imperfect body that Earthly parents knowingly or unknowingly created.

The greatest Real Truth® of all is that the universe, and all things found throughout the universe, have always existed. There was *never* a time when *nothing* existed ... and there will *never* be a time when *nothing* exists. The other great thing to know is that you can exist for as long as you want and live anywhere in this universe ... worlds without end ... as long as you do not cause other people to feel uncomfortable with your presence.

Again, the authors of this book are True Messengers. One day, we will reveal all that we know. We will make this information available to you free of charge. You might be able to buy anything in this world for money, but what is *really* valuable to your *eternal soul* will always be free. We cannot charge you for something that we didn't create. The Real Truth® is, was, and will always be *things as they really* are ... worlds without end. Our final book, our final attempt to share all that we know with the people of this world, will be called:

The Dream of Mortal Life, Understanding Human Reality—A Sharp Two-edged Sword, A FINAL WARNING to the Human Race.

Until we reveal more details about human reality in this final book, we hope that the book you are reading serves you in helping you make your own decision of whether or not to end your life upon Earth. You can make the choice to continue to live and experience things by acting upon these things, and being acted upon by these things, according to your own free will.

Before you can make the *proper* choice, a choice that will serve your unique desires of happiness, we are confident that we have revealed enough of the Real Truth® about ...

Suicide and the Eternal Nature of the Soul.

Chapter 10

Real Truth® Summary

Who We Are and Why We Exist

There is only one way to understand Real Truth®—things as they *really* were in the past, as they *really* are in the present, and as they *really* will be in the future: EMPIRICAL, PHYSICAL EVIDENCE.

No matter how nuanced (varied) and wonderful human imagination might be, when actual human consciousness and existence is taken out of the equation of rational thought, what is imagined will never be part of Real Truth®.

There are no life forms greater than human beings. There never have been and there never will be ... worlds without end. If time travel were possible, one would find that human beings, *always* and without exception, are the greatest life form that exists anywhere in the universe. The EMPIRICAL, PHYSICAL EVIDENCE of what we have experienced on this earth proves this, without exception.

There has never been a time, and there never will be, when a dolphin, a raven, or a chimpanzee learned how to control the power of the atom to serve the needs and wants of its own species. These species are widely celebrated as intelligent, yet they could not care less about anything other than their own existence. Furthermore, they do not have the mental capacity to control the physical elements of the environment in which they exist.

ONLY humans use reason, complex language skills, and introspection of their own existence, as well as logical contemplation of the existence of all other life forms around them. If human science is correct, then the human species is the *only* species that has evolved intellectually.

Science *imagines* (theorizes) that humans have evolved over time. From *Homo habilis* (tool-making and -using man) to the more modern *Homo sapiens* (wise man), it is widely *imagined* that if we were to travel far enough back in time, we would encounter our grunting, uncivilized, human-like ancestors.

What's interesting, though, is that science allows our *imagination* to visualize future humans living in advanced societies. We base these *theories* about the future solely on the empirical, physical evidence that exists on Earth today. If science would humble itself and apply the same observations of our current world by analyzing the EMPIRICAL, PHYSICAL EVIDENCE—*only* what we can see, hear, taste, smell, and touch—it would *imagine* the Real Truth® about our ancient ancestors.

As mentioned earlier in this book, we will publish a book in the future titled *The Dream of Mortal Life, Understanding Human Reality—A Sharp Two-edged Sword, A Final Warning to the Human Race*. This book will be completely *free* to all of Earth's inhabitants. It will provide the most rational and comprehensive information, proving that humans are, have been, and always will be the most advanced compendium of matter possible. It will provide logical arguments that there have always been humans living on planet Earth throughout its many billions of years of existence. It will give sound evidence that there have been five different *dispensations of human time* where humans were at least as advanced (and, in most of these times, much more advanced) as they are today (the time period recognized as the 21st Century).

Unfortunately, if you decide to end your life upon Earth, you will not have this incredible information to either dissuade or persuade you in your life-ending decision. Therefore, now, while you're still alive, we hope to provide you with some simple and clear information that sums up what this future book will explain in detail. Again, to arrive at an understanding of Real Truth®, we must base this information on EMPIRICAL, PHYSICAL EVIDENCE ... what a person can see, hear, taste, smell, and touch. We hope this brief summary helps you in your decision.

One of two things will happen if you commit suicide: 1) you will become unconscious and never exist again, or 2) you will become aware that you continue to be conscious—yet in another, completely different, plane of existence. If the former (first listed above) is true, your life experience upon Earth is futile and useless. If the latter is true—and we can assure you that it is the Real Truth®—the YOU that exists outside of this earth's environment is *not* the same human being who is conscious while experiencing life on this earth.

Our universe is the *only* plane of existence or dimension of any kind. *Consciousness* can only occur when one physically exists on one of the numberless planets found throughout this eternal (without beginning or end) physical plane. In our universe, a "plane" is a surface of matter that continues in all directions. This *matter* (what it is made of) is currently known as *dark matter*, or the infinite cosmos of space.

How Humans Travel Throughout the Universe

When you end your *earth experience*, you will *instantaneously* be aware that the *real YOU* is living as a conscious human on another planet in this exact same universe. The *real YOU*— hereinafter referred to as the *only* "you"—is not going to wonder *how* you traveled from Earth back to this planet. You did *not* take a space ship. You did *not* ride on a comet. You will realize that your physical body never actually left this planet. Once conscious (after your mortal death), you will be aware that this post-mortal existence was actually your *only* existence all along. You will then have the proof of how *all* advanced humans, without exception, travel throughout the universe.

Humans travel great distances by connecting their consciousness to what we have called throughout this book the *WIRELESS INTERGALACTIC INTERNET SERVICE*. There is *no other way* that a human being can travel these infinite distances, while keeping their physical body, with its brain's consciousness, intact. (We explained how this occurs in Chapter 3.)

FIRST STATE of Human Conscious Existence

How you were created and became a conscious, living human, ties in with how you can travel throughout the endless universe instantaneously. Your physical brain is made out of the same *matter* as the rest of the universe. Being of the same physical build, whatever happens to this construct, also happens to you at the exact same time it happens to everything else that exists in this construct (the universe).

When a (premortal) *human* physical body is created, it is created differently from all other life forms. The coding of the physical structure of the brain allows for the uniqueness of human existence compared to all other life forms. The human brain operates (acts upon and reacts to) within *dark matter* differently from all other brains of all other life forms. Each life form has a central processing unit (CPU) that creates the unique consciousness and abilities of that particular life form.

Consider how fast Internet connections are today compared to how slow they were just a few years in the past. Now consider how fast these connections could be if the CPU of the human brain was as advanced as it could possibly be. *Imagining* this will help you understand, not only how fast you can connect to other human bodies existing anywhere in the universe, but also how incredible having a highly advanced *human CPU* could be (and is).

Most advanced humans cannot create new, highly advanced human bodies ... new human CPUs ... because their own CPU does not have the knowledge, nor the physical ability, to create a new human being. Those who can do this are known as *Creators*. Creators (special advanced humans) live in solar systems that allow them the ability to create other new bodies. The *glory of these Creators is INTELLIGENCE*.

Our current solar system only allows humans to use machines to help them create new *things* (such as a synthetic diamond or a sapphire). However, no machine that is invented in this solar system will ever be able to take raw *dark matter* and create a new, advanced human person. Although the dark matter is the same throughout the universe, the *intelligence* to manipulate and use dark matter is controlled and restricted in all solar systems. ONLY Creators have the intelligence, the ability, the "license," to create any *thing* from raw dark matter.

A Creator created the perfect physical body for you. With this body, and existing in your Creator's solar system, you had the ability to connect your brain to *any* part of the universe instantaneously, without leaving your *home planet*. In this way, as it has been explained to you in this book, you were able to develop from infancy into adulthood. An advanced human body matures to a specific age and then does not age further. In this advanced body, you could create your own unique life experiences. All of these new experiences were and are stored in your own advanced, *human RAM* (random-access memory). This advanced *RAM* is as limitless as dark matter itself.

As you have new experiences, your brain stores them, physically. However, a stored experience cannot be remembered without the *same* energy that exists throughout the universe as dark matter. A human brain needs to be physical. Its incredible setup allows you to have and record an infinite number of experiences.

Keep in mind that, unlike brains, modern computers are *not* organic (living). These machines (robots, for example) are made of inorganic (non-living) materials. No matter how advanced, an inorganic machine cannot do what an organic life form can. Life allows the continuation of creation without limitations, while inorganic matter is restricted to its physical limitations. In other words, a living human brain is constantly expanding its energy. *Living energy* is a lot different from a non-living element that cannot create extra capacity for itself. (This concept will not be explained in detail here.)

There are actually three kinds of matter: 1) inorganic (non-living, like a robot or computer); 2) restricted (animals, plants, and all other living organisms); and 3) unrestricted. ONLY humans can be unrestricted. However, most humans do have restrictions placed on their brains and on their bodies. There are only two types of humans who possess a totally unrestricted brain capacity: 1) Creators (females) and 2) Overseers (males).

SECOND STATE of Human Conscious Existence

Once you had lived a very long time, and had visited as many solar systems throughout the universe as you desired, you eventually determined what kind of existence you wanted for yourself. You experienced many different types of human existences as you developed as a newly created human being. You knew that you had made a self-determined decision of what kind of human you wanted to be, because you began to have the same experiences over and over again. After having the same type of experiences over and over again, you came to the realization that you had found your *humanity type*.

Once you made this determination, you no longer desired to live in your *Creator's* solar system. You did not like it. Creators give up their free will of exploring the universe, in order to create other humans who *do* explore. You desired to live among other humans who had made the same determination as you.

Although Creators (females) have the *intelligence* to create new human bodies, they do not use this intelligence to create new solar systems (which combine with other solar systems and eventually become galaxies). *Overseers* (males) are the only humans who have the intelligence to create new solar systems.

Once you made the determination of your own *humanity type*, you either joined others in their established solar system, or you had an Overseer create a new one that fit your determined desires more appropriately. Because you did not want to live alone in this newly created solar system, you wanted many others to join you in it.

You were first created with a body that was able to exist in your Creator's unique solar system (**First State of Existence/First Estate**). Once you made your selection for your new life adventures, you had to leave your Creator's solar system. The body that was originally made for you no longer served the purpose for your continued existence. A new body, specifically designed for your new chosen solar system, was created. This is called the **Second State of Your Existence**.

In every solar system that exists in the universe, there are Creators assigned for each. These Creators create the type of bodies that are compatible for each solar system. This physical compatibility includes the restrictions placed on the body, depending on each solar system's unique restrictions. Because these Creators live in these solar systems, they do *not* create the same type of body that you had in your *First Estate*. (In this book, we will not detail the different restrictions placed on the different physical bodies created for the different *humanity types*. This will be done in the future book mentioned above.)

The new body that was created for your conscious experience in the *Second Estate* included the physical blueprint taken from the brain of the body you had in your *First Estate*. In this way, you retained all of the past experiences you had in your *First Estate*. (This is similar to how your Earth parents passed on the blueprints of their brains to you here. However, earthlings inherit the actual experiences of their parents, many of which a new infant would *not* opt for, if given the choice.)

Unlike your mortal body, the body you have in the *Second Estate* is unadulterated by other experiences, outside of those you accumulated in the *First Estate*. The new experiences of your *Second Estate* are added to those that you will have forever more. Furthermore, other than the restrictions of not being a Creator or an Overseer, your *Second Estate brain's CPU* and *RAM* are very similar to the power of your *First Estate brain's* physical makeup.

It is in the *Second Estate* that you can live forever, as long as YOU want, with the restrictions placed upon the *humanity type* that you chose for yourself. In this state of consciousness, you are well aware of the existence of *Creators* and *Overseers* and the difference between YOU and them.

THIRD STATE of Human Conscious Existence

There are some people existing in the *Second Estate* who, over a long period of time, began to wonder why they should be restricted in their *intelligence*. Their restriction took place because they chose a humanity type that did not allow them the power and intelligence of Creators and Overseers. Their personal pride got the best of them and they started questioning whether they made the right choice for themselves when they transitioned from the *First Estate* to the *Second*. This *pride* started to cause a few problems among other people who did not question their decision.

There are special solar systems set up for these questioners. They can connect their consciousness to these particular planets in order to see how they would act, *if* given power over others.

Creators and *Overseers* have a lot ... a whole lot ... of power (intelligence) over others. These are allowed to hold this kind of omnipotence because they have been tried and tested to see what they would do if they *did* have power over others. How did they use their power to affect the free will of another human being? Did they put *their* free will above another's? Creators and Overseers are *servers*. They exist to make sure you have what you desire, as long as what you desire does not impede the free-willed desires of others.

This Earth, in this solar system, is one of these special places where a person can have a temporary experience and test their free will against a Creator's and an Overseer's.

Keep in mind that the measure of a person's ability to experience happiness is fixed to their humanity type. A person who has an *earth experience* will judge themselves based on what made them happy during their mortal life experience, and what did not. In the pursuit of their happiness, did they do something, or not do something, that impeded or affected the happiness of another person? It's a simple judgment. It's a judgment that each of Earth's inhabitants will make about the experiences they had while living on Earth. While here on Earth, they do not have the same restrictions they are subject to in their chosen *Second Estate*.

This *earth experience* allows events to happen that *never* happen in a solar system with *Second Estate* restrictions. In a *Second Estate*, there are no animals or plants, of any kind, that kill or hurt. All animals serve the happiness of those who exist in these solar systems. In contrast, on Earth there are humans who protect animals that hurt and kill others. These humans are *happy* to conserve the existence of predators that kill humans, if given the chance.

There is no money on a *Second Estate* planet. Upon Earth, there are humans who are happy that they have enough money to serve their own needs and wants. They take no interest in what having money does to those who don't. They are not concerned with how their money is accumulated. These humans are *happy* to be provided for, or to provide for only those who make them *happy*.

There are no leaders in a *Second Estate*, because there is no one living there that needs someone to tell them what to do and how to do it. There is no government. People know how to act and act appropriately. There is no popularity. There is no person who is accepted as successful, popular, achieved, or blessed. All see as they are seen and know as they are known.

There are no family units or "loved ones" in the *Second Estate*. How can there be, when the inhabitants of these solar systems *chose* to be there and associate with the people of their own choosing? On Earth, what would you do for your family or loved ones? Whose happiness, whose life, would you affect (either in action or inaction), in support of your own family and loved ones?

We could go on for pages explaining how the *earth experience* was set up perfectly to allow people to connect to the mortal experience and prove themselves. ALL who come to Earth learn that they cannot be trusted to pursue and satisfy their happiness without affecting the happiness of other humans. They will be their own judges. They will know that nobody forced them to act in pursuit of their own happiness by affecting the happiness of another. But they will know that they did (affect the happiness of others in pursuit of their own). They will know that, in so doing, it made them happy.

"Time Travel"

Throughout the universe, there are an infinite number of solar systems where humans live and pursue their own unique desires of happiness. With the bodies provided in our *First* and *Second Estates*, we are able to go anywhere we want in the universe, traveling anywhere we choose, as explained above.

There are many different worlds developing similarly to how this Earth developed. (Upon *this* Earth, during this *Third Estate*, humans have the ability to create other humans, although not in an advanced way.)

In your *First* and *Second Estates*, if you want to travel to any particular time period that occurred on Earth, you simply need to connect your consciousness to a particular earth that is experiencing a similar time period. This is the only way that a semblance of traveling backward or forward in time is possible.

There are many people currently existing on this earth whose *True Selves* are from a wide variety of solar systems. These want to experience what life is like here. As an example, let's say these people in the *Second Estate* want to experience the 2nd Century. If they already lived on Earth during the 2nd Century, they cannot travel back in time to be the person they were then. This type of time travel is impossible. Once an experience has occurred in one of your lifetimes, you cannot travel back to un-experience or change what you did or how you acted.

However, with an advanced human *CPU* and *RAM*, you can simply think about your past experiences and relive these experiences as if they are happening for the very first time ... EXACTLY LIKE YOU ARE LIVING YOUR CURRENT EXPERIENCE UPON THIS EARTH.

Your *True Eternal Self* is who you are. YOU exist in what we call the *Second Estate of Human Consciousness*. While you are reading this book, you will *not* know if you are reading this book for the very first time in the *Third Estate*, or if you are re-experiencing the event in your advanced brain in the *Second*.

There is a sure and easy way to tell. But this way will not be revealed in this book. If we were to tell you this way, the *earth experience* wouldn't be as meaningful to your *True Self.*

But this we *can* tell you:

If you commit suicide, your *True Self* will know that you once made that decision for yourself on this Earth; and this decision is something that you will never be able to change.

So, as you contemplate ending your life, think about *why* you are here on this earth having the life experience that you are having. Why did you come here in the first place? What were you trying to prove to yourself or to others? What if you knew the Real Truth® about who you are and why you exist?

What if you do take your life now and, one day, as an advanced human living in your eternal *Second Estate*, you desire to use your advanced brain's *CPU* and *RAM* to relive the experience just by thinking about it? At that point, looking back, do you think you would make the same decision, now that you know what you did and the consequence of what you did?

Only you can judge you.

Now you know the Real Truth® about ...

Suicide and the Eternal Nature of the Soul.

EPILOGUE

This book was not only meant for those who are contemplating suicide. As is often the case, there's not much that can be done for a person who is determined to end their own life. It is *why* they want to end their life that is of our greatest concern. This concern should also be foremost in the minds of people who know someone who is contemplating suicide.

Could it be that your relationship with them (the person who's contemplating suicide), how you've treated them, what you've said to them, and how they value their existence based on their relationship with you, contributed to their desire to commit suicide?

This world needs to change a lot of things about itself, if humanity wants to mitigate (lessen) the increasing instances of suicide, especially among the youth.

Adults, this book was *not* meant for the youth of this world. Few of them have the patience or desire to read it. But you can! You can consider the information presented herein, contemplate it carefully, and determine if this information might help you counsel your young loved one differently than the way they have been counseled and taught by you in the past.

If a child is considering suicide, it is usually because the adults in the child's life do not have the proper information needed to teach the child what the child needs to know, information that might create value and worth for the child's continued existence. As harsh as it might sound, adults are chiefly responsible for many of the reasons behind a young person's loss of hope that their existence is still worth something in this world.

We hope that this book helps the adults help the children.

We hope that this book will confront the PRIDE of the adult to consider the ego of the child.

We can do nothing but provide different and new information than that to which adults have been exposed. It is the current *adult information* that has *not* helped alleviate the youth suicide rate.

Adults, set your PRIDE aside for the moment. Do not let the blood of the youth of this world be on your hands!

LEARN FROM THIS BOOK!

www.ingramcontent.com/pod-product-compliance
Lightning Source LLC
Chambersburg PA
CBHW072139270326
41931CB00010B/1810